# Handpulled Rickshaw : A heritage of Calcutta

*Author*

**Dr. Dalia Ray**

M.A., L.L.B., Ph.D.

PUNTHI PUSTAK

KOLKATA : 2025

***Published by :***

Sirshendu Bhattacharya
**PUNTHI PUSTAK**
*Publisher, Bookseller & Exporter*
136/4B, Bidhan Sarani,
Kolkata - 700 004
Phone : 033-2555 5573, 9831318787
E-mail : punthipustak@hotmail.com

**1st Edition : January 1, 2025**



**ISBN : 978-93-81209-52-3**

**Price : Rs.495/-**

***Printed at :***
Kolkata

# CONTENTS

*Dedicated to late P.T. Nair, Calcutta historian and my revered mentor.*

# PREFACE

Hand pulled rickshaw, an important part of Calcutta's heritage, culture and transport system, is a very interesting subject for exploration and research. Being a research scholar I could not resist the temptation of researching on this subject which is a very relevant and current topic in the present context of the introduction of very modernised modes of transport in this City of Joy.

Calcutta, a city of contradictions, is today one of the few cities in the world where hand pulled rickshaws are still plying in the lanes and by-lanes of the city as a public mode of cheap transport. The hand rickshaw pullers, in fact form an integral part of the workforce as the hand rickshaws provide work and livelihood to the migrant workers from Bihar, Orissa, U.P., to the vulnerable urban dwellers as well as to the rural people of West Bengal, who are poor, illiterate, unskilled and unemployed. A handpulled rickshaw is a mode of human powered slow moving vehicle. It is a light wooden cart with two large wheels, also made of wood, along with a seat for two passengers, pulled by a man running between two long shafts that project in the front. The handrickshaw was first seen in Simla in the summer capital of British Raj in 1880. But it was first introduced in Calcutta in 1914 by the Chinese people living in this city, as a private means of transport for the purpose of carrying goods and for passenger transport. The first handrickshaws in Calcutta were not only owned by the Chinese residents but they were also pulled by the Chinese immigrants. By 1920s the rickshaw trade was almost Indianised. Surprisingly, Calcutta, historically the capital of British India, is one of the cities in the world which has still now retained handpulled rickshaw as a mode of public transport along with modernised fast moving mechanised modes of transport like the public bus, state bus, four wheelers, three wheeler autorickshaw and the Metro Railway. Above all, the handpulled rickshaw is pollution free and cheapest transport and the only means of transport in the waterlogged streets of Calcutta as they navigate through the serpentine lanes of Calcutta where neither a four wheeler nor a three wheeler car can enter. Thus the handpulled rickshaw is an icon of this metropolis and a permanent feature of Calcutta's traditional aura. The handrickshaw also continues to fascinate the foreign visitor to this City of Joy.

The questions raised in this study are limited to a few. How the ban imposed on hand rickshaw by the amendment of the Calcutta Hackney Carriage Act, 1919 has adversely affected the hand rickshaw pullers, owners, hand rickshaw craftsmen and the rickshaw trade as a whole as well as the problems like low income, unemployment and trade insecurity which the hand rickshaw pullers and owners have been facing for a long time since the year 2006 when the Kolkata Municipal Corporation had stopped issuing new licences to the rickshaw pullers and owners nor renewing the existing licences. But above all, the question of rehabilitation of the hand rickshaw pullers and owners has not yet been solved by the state government though it is high time that the state government treats this issue as urgent and solve the same. Otherwise a large number of pullers, who are out of work, will starve to death, along with their families since these pullers are unskilled for any other kind of work and they have no stake at their native place to fall back upon.

This book contains six chapters. The historical background leading to the introduction of handpulled rickshaw in Calcutta has been discussed in the first chapter. In the second chapter the life style of the hand rickshaw pullers, the rickshaw business, its utility and its hazards have been discussed. The third chapter highlights the history and activities of the various rickshaw associations and rickshaw unions in Calcutta. In chapter four there is an elaborate discussion on the present hand rickshaw pullers, owners and rickshaw craftsmen who are still involved in the rickshaw trade in Calcutta. Chapter five deals with the laws relating to the rickshaw trade as well as the litigations arising out of the problems faced by the pullers and owners. Finally the findings of my research study of the hand pulled rickshaws have been discussed in chapter six, viz the last chapter of this work. In the conclusion I have discussed about the issue of rehabilitation of the handrickshaw pullers and owners. It is high time that the State Government should take effective steps for rehabilitation of the pullers and owners by introducing e-rickshaws, in respect of which a draft resolution was made by the Transport Authority called Gatidhara Type-2 package for rehabilitation. But the said resolution was never put into effect. As regards the question as to whether hand rickshaws should be banned, my observation is that banning the hand rickshaw will create more problem in the public life of Calcutta, as over 2000 rickshaw pullers and also rickshaw craftsman will be out of work while the rickshaw owners will also suffer financially if hand rickshaw trade is banned. The hand rickshaws being pollution free, convenient and cheapest mode of transport, well suited to the transport needs of the Calcutta public at large, have been rendering valuable service to the Calcutta society at large, being reliable transport for carrying school children to and from home and school, being the only mode of transport in monsoon when the city's roads and lanes are waterlogged, reliable for carrying patients, old and sick as well as reliable for carrying goods. Furthermore banning the rickshaws will impoverish the pullers, owners and craftsmen. These handrickshaws, plying in Calcutta for more than a century have become a remarkable heritage of Calcutta which should be preserved for the posterity, as a token of non-motorised mode of transport and e-rickshaws should be introduced by the Government for the purpose of rehabilitation and for providing alternative work to the pullers and owners.

This work is based on the interview technique, field study and supplemented by archival sources, books, journals and newspapers.

The author acknowledges the help and co-operation of the office bearers of the All Bengal Rickshaw Union (ABRU), specially the help, cooperation and valuable assistance of Mr. Mukhtar Ali, the General Secretary of ABRU who was kind enough to sit for interview several times and spared his valuable time to inform the author about the past and present activities of ABRU and the problems which the rickshaw pullers and owners are facing today. Thanks are also due to the staff of the National Library, Calcutta, the West Bengal

State Archives, and the Kolkata Police Museum and Archives. Above all, the author expresses her thanks to all the present handrickshaw pullers, owners, sardars and rickshaw craftsmen in Calcutta who were kind enough to spare their working time and sit for interview in order to share their experiences in the rickshaw trade as well as their problems and grievances in their respective field of work.

The photographs exhibited in this book were taken by the author herself.

The author is sanguine that discerning readers will bear with her for the shortcomings of this work.

Dr. Dalia Ray
21/1/C, Ballygunge Station Road
Calcutta – 700019
31.10.2024

# Chapter I

## Introduction and Historical Background

Calcutta, a city of contradictions is now one of the few cities in the world where handpulled rickshaws (called tana rickshaws in Bengali) are still a mode of public transport. In fact, Calcutta is, at present, the only metropolis in India where hand rickshaw pullers form an integral part of the workforce and there is no denying the fact that handpulled rickshaws provide an opportunity for livelihood to the most vulnerable urban dwellers and migrant workers from Bihar, Orissa and Uttar Pradesh who are unskilled and unemployed. A handpulled rickshaw is a mode of human powered and slow moving vehicle by which a puller pulls a two wheeled rickshaw which seats one or two persons.

In medieval India and also during the British rule of India, human powered vehicle in the form of palki (palanquin) existed, which may be regarded as the forerunner of handpulled rickshaw. The palki was a covered carriage containing a seat for one or two persons, enclosed by curtains and it was carried by four persons on their shoulders, two on the front and two on the back of the palki. Even in the British era a large number of migrant workers from Bihar and Orissa served as palki bearers in the 18th and 19th centuries. But the use of palkis diminished and later on stopped permanently with the arrival of other modes of personal transport like horse-drawn carriages, bicycles, handpulled rickshaws, trams, railways and other forms of mechanised public transport[1].

The Hand Rickshaw or Jin-Riki-Sha in Japanese, (Jin meaning human, Riki meaning power and Sha meaning vehicle) literally meaning "man-powered vehicle" was first invented in Japan in 1869 and was introduced in China by 1874. Its invention has been credited to three persons namely Jonathan Gable, an American Missionary, Ahika Daisuki and a Japanese, Samurai Yusuke Tzumi. It is a light wooden cart with two large wheels, also made of wood, a seat for two passengers drawn by a man running between two long shafts that project in front. The vehicle was a major advance over the Sedan Chair or the Palanquin found in the 19th century Europe and Asia. Within a decade of its invention, the hand rickshaw was first seen in Simla in the hills of north India, the summer capital of the British Raj in 1880[2]. This fact is evident from Lady Dufferin's Memoirs[3]. About 20 years later the hand rickshaw was introduced in Calcutta for the carriage of goods as a private means of transport by the Chinese people living in this metropolis. In the year 1914 hand pulled rickshaws were plying for hire with Chinese pullers, for in this year the Chinese immigrants secured permission from the Municipal Corporation of Calcutta to operate rickshaws for passenger transport. The first Calcutta rickshaws were not only owned by Chinese residents, they were also pulled by the Chinese immigrants. By 1920s the rickshaw trade was almost completely Indianised[4]. It is also evident from the archival records that as early as 1932 another kind of handpulled rickshaw called the "Hongkong rickshaw" were imported into Calcutta by Messrs. Hoo Aik & Company having its office at No.67, China Street, Rangoon but residing at 3, Amratolla Street, Calcutta. This Company in Rangoon was the sole manufacturer and proprietor of this new type of rickshaws. This company imported ten rickshaws into Calcutta and these rickshaws were one seater rickshaws[4a].

Yea Lipcheang, the Manager and Constituted Attorney of Messrs Aik & Company submitted an application to the Deputy Commissioner of Police, Public Vehicles Department, Calcutta, praying for a declaration that this one seater rickshaws were fit and suitable for passengers for hire under the Police Regulations in Calcutta and Howrah[4b].

The Deputy Commissioner of Police, Public Vehicles Department, in reply, informed the Manager and Constituted Attorney of Messrs. Hoo Aik & Company, C/o. Messrs. Heap Thye & Company, 3, Amratolla Street, Calcutta, that the "Hongkong rickshaw" which was produced for inspection at this department, did not comply with the specification laid down by the Government of Bengal. Rickshaws for use in Calcutta must be capable for sitting two adult passengers and rates for rickshaws were fixed accordingly. Hongkong rickshaw was therefore not acceptable under the rules[4c]. Thus historically speaking the hand rickshaw is one of the oldest vehicles and mode of transport in the City of Joy.

Surprisingly Calcutta is the only city which has retained handpulled rickshaw still now along with the present day modernized transport like the Metro Railway. The long parallel shafts, and colourful seats with the "tung tang" sound of the metallic bells make the handpulled rickshaw a part of Calcutta's tradition, heritage and culture[5].

Hand rickshaw pullers form a part of the informal sector's work force in the city. These rickshaws are a cheap means of transportation and have provided employment to a large number of poor and illeterate unskilled labourers mostly from Bihar, Orissa and Uttar Pradesh. Almost 80% of the rickshaw pullers have migrated to Calcutta from Bihar, leaving their families behind in their native places. These people have migrated from the districts of Gaya, Jahanabad, Muzaffarpur, Darbhanga, Samastipur, Bhagalpur, Mungyer, Giridih or Chapra in Bihar. 11% have migrated from other Indian states like Orissa and U.P. and also from the neighbouring country of Bangladesh. The remaining 9% hails from rural West Bengal[6]. Even today Calcutta's hand rickshaw pullers are mainly outsiders from the neighbouring and even more poverty stricken state of Bihar[7].

Handpulled rickshaws still exist as tourist attraction or historical oddities in very small number in many cities of the world. The historic city of Kurashiki in Japan has a few ready to be posed for photographs and in Hong Kong, a few hang around by the Star Ferry wharf on Hong Kong Island. A few number of rickshaws also are still seen in the lanes of Hanoi, Vietnam, Penang, Jakarta and Cambodia. But only in Calcutta handpulled rickshaws are still in everyday use as a mode of transport[8].

During the 1920s and 1930s the city's rickshaw fleet expanded rapidly, even though the number of rickshaws was declining in other cities of the world. In 1939 the city authorities decreed an absolute maximum of 6000 licences but after World War II the rickshaw population continued to grow. The combination of poverty, congestion and a ban on cycle rickshaws in Calcutta city center encouraged the handpulled rickshaw's number to increase to around 50,000 in the 1980s[9].

Around the year, 2003, there were an estimated 18,000 rickshaw pullers in Calcutta operating in Shyambazar, Hatibagan, Shovabazar, Bowbazar, College Street, Burrabazar, Sealdah, Taltala, Moulali, Amherst Street, Hogg Market (New Market), Bhowanipur, Kalighat, Gariahat, Ballygunge and Kidderpore. Handpulled rickshaws stand out as the most convenient and cheapest transport in this city, particularly during monsoon when the roads and by-lanes of Calcutta are waterlogged. Many of this rickshaw pullers who sleep on the city's streets also serve as a 24 hours emergency ambulance service when required. Many of them take children to school daily on a monthly basis. Handpulled rickshaws also serve another important purpose viz carrying goods and luggages of people from one place to another[10].

***Notes and References***

1. Ghosal, Soumya Sarkar, an article on handpulled rickshaws published on 9th December, 2019 (www.sahapedia.org).
2. The Calcutta Samaritans & Action Aid, Kolkata, A Report on Hand Rickshaw Pullers of Kolkata, 2003, Kolkata, p.5, Ghoshal, Soumya Sarkar, www.sahapedia.org, 9th December, 2019.
3. Siddiqui, M.K.A. (ed) Aspects of Society and culture in Calcutta, Article, "The Rickshawallas and the Thelawallas in Calcutta, by Asim Maitra, Calcutta, 1982, p.197.
4. The Calcutta Samaritans & Action Aid, Kolkata, op. cit, p.5.

4a. Proceedings of the Government of Bengal, Police Department, September, 1933, File No. Plo-H-2(1) of 1932, dated Rangoon, 1st August, 1932, State Archives, Calcutta.

4b. Proceedings of the Government of Bengal, Police Department, September, 1933, File No. Plo-M-Z(1) of 1932 dt. Rangoon, 1st August, 1932 State Archives, Calcutta.

4c. Proceedings of the Government of Bengal, Police Department, September, 1933, File No.69 H.C.B. dated Calcutta, 19th July, 1932, State Archives, Calcutta.

5. The Calcutta Samaritans & Action Aid, Kolkata, op.cit., p.5.

6. The Calcutta Samaritans & Action Aid, Kolkata, op.cit. pp.5, 11.

7. Wheeler, Tony & Anson, Richard 1, 'Chasing Rickshaws', Australia, 1998.

8. Wheeler Tony & Anson'1, Richard, op.cit.

9. Wheeler Tony & Anson'l, Richard, op.cit.

10. A report on handpulled rickshaws of Kolkata by the Calcutta Samaritans & Action Aid, op.cit., pp.6-7.

# Chapter II

## Life style of the Hand rickshaw pullers, the rickshaw business, its utility and its hazards

Rickshawalla is an occupational name given to the people who earn their livelihood by pulling rickshaw in Calcutta. Rickshaw pulling is unskilled and requires no educational attainment or formal training as such. The handpulled rickshawallas are originally poor villagers, mainly from Bihar and U.P. who have migrated to Calcutta for the purpose of employment. Most of these rickshawallas are illeterate and low caste people. Almost all the rickshaw pullers are Biharis who have left their families in their native villages and spend most of their time in Calcutta to earn an income. All these handpulled rickshaws are mostly owned by Biharis, Bengalies and a few by Punjabis and Marwaries. The owners of this rickshaws are mainly middle class people like shopkeepers, clerks and teachers who purchase and maintain a few rickshaws as a source of extra income. But there are some people who own large number of rickshaws and rickshaw business is their only source of income. Generally no rickshaw puller owns a rickshaw. There are Sardars who act as middlemen between the owners and the pullers. The duties of these Sardars are to maintain the rickshaw properly and to collect the hire-money from the puller[1].

**Who are the handrickshaw pullers? their origin :**

According to a survey on hand rickshawpullers made in 1982 it was found that muslims and low caste hindus form the majority among the rickshawpullers in Calcutta. Mr. Asim Maitra in his survey, did not find any Brahmin or a tribal person to pull the rickshaw. Among the muslims, Sheikh, Momin, Pathan, Sabzifrosh are generally found in rickshaw pulling. Of them Sheikh and Sabzifrosh of Darbhanga and Monghyr districts predominate in number. Among the hindus the various castes involved in rickshaw pulling are Goala, Dosadh, Musahar, Bhuiya, Chamar, Tili, Paswan, Rajput, Kahar, Kori, Mallah, Kumar, Kayastha, Mahisya, Namasudra, Pod and Banik. Thus the lower caste people including scheduled castes and O.B.C. from Bihar are mainly engaged in rickshaw pulling in Calcutta. According to a study in 1982 it was found that a very small percentage, around 22.5% are literate viz they can sign their name in Hindi. The remaining of them are illiterate. Majority of them are married. Their age varies from 15 to 65 years[2].

These rickshawallas are not permanent dwellers in the city but originally they are villagers from different parts of India who have temporarily migrated to Calcutta in search of work. Extreme poverty drives them out of their home. They come to Calcutta and joins this urban profession mainly through their relatives and known persons who are already in this business of rickshaw pulling. Thus economic factors like poverty and unemployment drive these low caste poor people to leave their native villages and come to Calcutta in the hope of earning an income for their own and their family members' subsistence and survival.

Inspite of the different positions of their ethnic groups, many rickshawallas are engaged in agricultural work in their villages. In other words, those who are born in agricultural family, agriculture is their primary occupation while rickshawpulling is subsidiary occupation. Many of them possess agricultural land. A large number of them are found pursuing this subsidiary occupation for three generations (grand-father, father and son)[3].

**Life style of the Rickshaw pullers :**

As a rickshawpuller joins this occupation through his known persons or relatives who are already persuing this profession in Calcutta, it is also pre-decided where and with whom the new comer will stay in Calcutta. His relatives give him all sorts of training in pulling a rickshaw. When he gets full training as a puller, his relatives bring him before the rickshaw pullers and owners' union for obtaining a rickshaw pulling licence or directly applying for a licence in the Hackney Carriage department of the Government of West Bengal. Thereafter he procures a rickshaw from an owner of the locality where he resides[4].

The rickshawallas reside in slums, dilapidated houses, rickshaw garages or khatals and on the pavements of the city where they park their rickshaws at night. Sometimes they hire a room for kitchen purpose and sleep on the pavements. They usually use common toilets situated in different markets or also beside roads. Sometimes some of the rickshawallas are fortunate to get free accommodation in an outhouse of a landlord or of a rickshaw owner, to guard their houses at night.

Some of the rickshaw owners also make arrangements for the stay of their own rickshaw pullers in their rickshaw garages. It is generally an open space with tin and tiles shaded roof with pucca floor. Sometimes the rickshawallas also reside in rooms made of mud walls and mud floor with small tiled roof known as kachha house in a slum[5].

As the hand rickshawpullers live in the city without their families, often most of them live together in a joint mess. In this co-operative living the rickshaw pullers cook in one kitchen and share their duties of cooking, collecting water etc. A kitchen unit mainly consists of the members of the same caste. But different kitchen groups may live together in the same place or room. Among muslim rickshawpullers the pullers may belong to the same group as well as different ethnic groups of muslim community. It is also found that the members of a kitchen unit tend to be related by kinship, village brotherhood etc. and it is found that castes or groups hailing from the same village or from the same district tend to cluster together. Food of a rickshawpuller is very simple viz. rice, chattu, (mixture of grinding grain, maize and jowar), dal (lentils), vegetable curry and chilli chutney. Very rarely he can afford to eat fish, egg or meat as a special luxury[6].

The hand rickshawpullers do not possess any regular bed, beddings or cot. Their bedding consists of two chhots (hessian cloths), one wooden block used as a pillow, one blanket and very rarely one Khatia (viz a wooden or bamboo framed cot covered by a network of ropes)[7].

**Social and Economic implications**

The hand rickshaw trade has social and economic

implications. To the hand rickshawpullers it was never a desirable occupation but it was a compulsion as the economic needs of their respective families and their indigent condition have prompted them to take up this profession as this profession requires no skill, no extensive formal training or education. Most of these rickshawallas are homeless and have no agricultural land in their native villages. Some of them have followed in the footsteps of their hand rickshaw pulling forefathers[8].

The rickshaw trade is large-scale, informal and not very stable, though long-established. It employs 7 to 8% of the men[8a].

Due to lack of social consciousness and illiteracy, the family of the average hand rickshaw puller is rather big. The hand rickshawpuller community consisting of Yadavs (higher caste), Dalits, Harijans, other scheduled castes and muslims is secular in nature and is an example of rare harmony of the nearly 18000 pullers in the year 2003. Over 75% dwelt in 'deras' or places where they park their rickshaws at night. These 'deras' belong to the 'Sardars' who collect the hand rickshaws on rental basis from the owners and engage the pullers at different rates. Some owners also have rickshaw 'Khatals' or garages where the pullers park the rickshaws at night, provided that those rickshaws belong to those particular owners. The owners and sardars are the most privileged class in terms of economic viability in the 'owner-sardar-puller' triangle. There is no wage rule (or a rate card issued by the transport authorities), so that the pullers charge the passengers at an arbitrary rate. However traffic restriction has hit most of these vulnerable rickshawpullers as since 1996 if a rickshawpuller is caught by a policeman for violating a traffic rule like plying through certain roads which have been barred for handpulled rickshaw, the rickshawpuller has to pay Rs.75/- to Rs.100/- as a bribe to the policeman to get his vehicle out on the streets again[9].

The hand rickshawpullers form a part of the 40-50% informal sector work force in the city. But their work is hard and lowpaid and the pullers are poorly organised. But there is no denying the fact that handpulled rickshaw trade provides a livelihood opportunity to the poor migrants from Bihar, Orissa and U.P. who are illeterate and unskilled[10].

**Categories of pullers and their earnings**

In Calcutta there are two categories of hand rickshawpullers — part-time pullers and whole-time pullers. A puller who pulls the rickshaw for both day and night is known as a whole-time rickshawpuller (viz. from early morning to noon and from late afternoon till night). The part-time rickshawpullers usually work from early morning to late afternoon but their number is large than the whole-time pullers. The part-time pullers, before or after pulling rickshaws, also do some subsidiary jobs such as water lifting in a house, or as an escort of school children or as a load carrier or as a taxi cleaner with the sole object of earning an extra income[11].

The earnings of the hand rickshawpullers are not fixed. Their earnings and expenditure varies according to the location of their operation. The pullers operating in the 'posh' areas of the city like Ballygunge, Gariahat, Bhowanipur or Kalighat earn more than their counterparts in Burrabazar, Sealdah, Taltala, Amherst Street or Kidderpore[12]. Irrespective of their earnings, they save a part of their earnings after deducting the cost of food and lodging. Their monthly savings are not fixed and their savings vary from Rs.30/- to 150/- per month. The money they save, they invest back at home to buy agricultural implements, and to cater to the needs of their family members[13]. The low earnings of the rickshawpullers vary between Rs.100/- to Rs.120/- a day on average. This low income places the pullers only a rung about the rag pickers and beggars of the city. The Calcutta hand rickshaw pullers are at or below the internationally recognised poverty levels. With this meagre income the rickshawpullers have to support their families (which on an average consists of 4-5 members). Each puller sends between Rs.1000/- to Rs.1500/ - to their families. What is left is spent for their own food, shelter, clothing and rental charges for their rickshaws. Their earnings are barely enough for their livelihood. Hence matters relating to education and health have to be relegated to the background. Almost all of them are illiterate with the exception of a few young people who have taken to rickshaw pulling for lack of anything better to do. Over 90% of them have no savings at all and are in debt[14].

## Occupational Hazards and Health Hazards

The hand rickshawpullers in Calcutta have almost no remedy for health problems. If they become ill, their survival is almost at stake. Most of them suffer from tuberculosis, arthiritis, bronchial asthma, malaria, lung disease, dermatological problems, sexually transmitted diseases and other infectious diseases. Many of them are addicted to chemical substances, country liquor, narcotics, and tobacco leaves (khainee and gutkha in hindi). The reasons behind such addiction are tensions of the trade, melancholia and living away from their families. A direct consequence of their feeling of loneliness is their visits to prostitutes or indulging in homo sextual practices. Their illeteracy and lack of awareness also cause them to become victims of HIV/AIDS and STD. In the event of falling sick, they borrow money from their fellow pullers or at times from the sardars for medical treatment. On average they spend 4-6% of their earnings for medical purpose. Majority of the pullers go for treatment only when it becomes unbearable. Mostly they seek treatment in government hospitals or clinics run by NGOs while many of them go to quacks, ayurveda consultants or homeopathic practitioners[15].

**Utility**

A non-motorised transport, the handpulled rickshaw of Calcutta is a pollution free vehicle. Pulling a rickshaw does not require any skill; it requires only hard physical labour. It provides employment for those who need it desperately to maintain their families in the villages. It is a cheap, reliable and consumer-friendly transport option in a city where buses are irredeemably dirty, crowded and dangerous and the car or taxi is unaffordable for the majority of the residents. They are particularly useful for women, the elderly, the frail and the disabled. The rickshawallas will serve customers at any hour of the day or night, will work during the worst of the monsoons and through the most waterlogged streets and will take children to and from the school in a city where personal care and reliability are highly valued. Every rickshaw journey is a journey which cannot be replaced by another form of transport since rickshaw journey is pollution free. Every rickshaw journey provides employment opportunities that are otherwise simply non-existent[16].

The hand rickshaw is primarily made of wood (betelnut wood for shafts and spokes, sisoo wood for hub and felloes, cheap hardwood for the body). But metal is used for fastenings, axle, bearing, spring, struts and in the form of galvanised sheet for covering the wooden body. The total weight is 80 to 90 kilogram. Shafts are straight and integral with the floor of the body. The centre of gravity is very high. Boarding and alighting involve a step height of 55 cm. The puller has considerable leverage for balancing and steering. There are no brakes, although sudden stopping is common. The hood may be lowered or raised against the sun or rain and supplemented by front and side curtains during heavy rain. There is space under the seat for storage of spanner, curtains and puller's possessions. The wheels are usually painted black and lined in red[16a].

The handpulled rickshaw plays an important role as a non-motorized transport in urban sustainability and development, since it reduces air pollution, provides income for the poor and also provides transport for the vulnerable groups. Thus non-motorized transport makes a substantial contribution to reducing air pollution simply by providing an alternative to heavily polluted motorized transport. So if handpulled rickshaws disappear from Calcutta's streets there would not only be increase in air pollution but also a substantial increase in the number of people living in poverty[17].

Moreover non-motorized transport offers significant benefits for low income groups, the sick, the elderly women and the children. This is particularly important in a developing country like India where so many people live in poverty. Non motorized transport is cheaper, non-polluting and more flexible as it provides employment to the unskilled and is labour intensive in terms of operation, manufacture and maintenance of vehicles[18].

The handpulled rickshaw can carry only two adults. Considering the physically demanding nature of rickshawpulling, the number of trips made per day is limited to 10/20 with an average of 15. As for distance travelled, most journeys are short and less than 2/3 kilometers[19].

Despite their age (they came into use in Calcutta a century ago), handpulled rickshaws continue to be used throughout the city and remain among the more heavily used systems of transport, by all types of people – householders, shopkeepers, businessmen, small manufacturers, school-children and as ambulances during emergency. Rickshaws are readily available at convenient locations at all times of day and night. They carry passengers close to their final destinations. They are available durign rush hours when other mode of transport are grossly overloaded and especially for movements in and through the dense neighbourhoods of central Calcutta. During heavy rain in Calcutta, the handpulled rickshaw is often the only mode of transport in the water logged streets. Children are sent to school by parents in the care of a trusted puller[20].

Goods carriage is a major activity of the hand pulled rickshaws near all the central markets, especially, Sealdah, Machuabazar and Posta. In a count of rickshaw movements in the early evening on Howrah Bridge, 70 percent of this rickshaws carry goods or bulky baggage. Rickshaws allow owners to travel with their load. Sometimes goods are carried unaccompanied. Rickshaws are ideally suited for petty tradesmen to carry small quantities of goods, not sufficient for tempos. Rickshaws are ideally suited for delivery of goods to small establishments in narrow lanes where most petty businesses and industries in Calcutta are located and are in some places the only vehicle that can travel in such areas. Passenger travel by rickshaw is cheaper than taxis for short distances. For goods carriage also hand pulled rickshaws are cheaper than other modes[21].

Compared to other modes of transport, handpulled rickshaws are cheaper and easy to maintain. Energy is purely manual and so it is labour intensive[22].

**Rickshaw owners and Rickshawpullers**

Surveys suggest that more than 90 percent of the pullers and owners come from Bihar and maintain a kind of dual residence in Calcutta and in their native villages. Of them majority are married and have families in their native places while very few of them have families living in the city. Very few pullers own their own vehicles – less than one in a hundred. The normal custom is that the puller rents his vehicle from the fleet of an owner or Sardar, on a shift basis. Many rickshaw pullers are either too poor or seasonal migrants plying the rickshaw only for a few months when their agricultural land back home lies fallow[23]. The owner takes responsibility for the cost of keeping the vehicle in service including payment for repairs, licensing and overnight garaging. Rickshaw owners are often people with considerable influence and interest in the trade is therefore vested. For example the president of the All Bengal Rickshaw Union (ABRU) was the Deputy Speaker of West Bengal Assembly. It has been heard that many members of the Calcutta Police have been owners of hand pulled rickshaw fleets[24].

**Licence for the hand pulled rickshaws**

There are four types of licences for the rickshaw trade – (1) the owner's licence previously issued by the Hackney Carriage Department, (2) Calcutta Corporation Licence (road tax), (3) Owner's trade or business licence issued by the Calcutta Municipal Corporation and (4) Puller's Licence (Hackney Carriage Act). The owner's licence is the most important but new licences have ceased being issued after 1939. No new vehicles are legally allowed to be manufactured; even old rickshaws are legally not allowed to be replaced by new ones. Vehicles renewal, however takes place by gradual removal and replacement of parts[25].

By an earlier law, viz. section 16 of the Calcutta Hackney Carriage Act, 1919, unlicensed vehicles were fined by the police with a fine not exceeding Rs.100/-. But after the amendment of this Act on May, 1980, rickshaw owners were liable to pay a fine of Rs.50/- to Rs.500/- or undergo three month's imprisonment.[26]

Remarkably all the official forms and certificates for licensing, registering and operating a rickshaw in Calcutta are in English. There is an annual registration fee of Rs.10/- and six monthly fee of Rs.15/- for keeping a rickshaw legally on the road. The expiry date of the registration is stenciled on the back of each rickshaw[27].

But accordingly to a report on the rickshaws, the licensing system is abused, it has turned out to be a mechanism for harassment and exploitation rather than regulation for either welfare or efficiency. Though the rickshaw pullers do not have any registration but their vehicles are registered[28]. But at present the entire situation has changed. Since the amendment of the Calcutta Hackney Carriage Act, no renewal or issuance of new licence has taken place since the year, 2006.

***Notes and References***

1. Siddique, M.K.A. (ed), Article, 'Aspects of Society & Culture in Calcutta', 1982 by Asim Maitra, pp.198-199, 213.
2. Siddique, M.K.A. (ed), op.cit., p.199.
3. Siddique, M.K.A. (ed), op.cit. p.215.
4. Siddique, M.K.A. (ed), op.cit., p.203.
5. Siddique, M.K.A. (ed), op.cit. pp. 202 – 203.
6. Siddinque, M.K.A. (ed), op.cit., pp. 208 – 209.
7. Siddique, M.K.A. (ed), op.cit., p. 210.
8. The Calcutta Samaritans & Action Aid, Kolkata, 'A Report on Hand rickshawpullers of Kolkata, 2003, Kolkata, p. 13.

8a. Thomas, T.H., 'Rickshaws in Calcutta', a report, February, 1981 (Unnayan AIIP, 36/1A, Garcha Road, Caclutta-19) p.30

9. The Calcutta Samaritans & Action Aid Kolkata, op.cit., pp. 13, 15
10. The Calcutta Samaritans & Action Aid, Kolkata, op.cit., p. 26
11. Siddique, M.K.A. (ed), Aspects of Society and Culture in Calcutta, article, 'The Rickshawallas and the Thelawallas in Calcutta' by Asim Maitra, p. 204.
12. The Calcutta Samaritans & Action Aid, Kolkata, op.cit., p. 16
13. Siddique, M.K.A. (ed), op.cit., p. 211
14. The Calcutta Samaritans & Action Aid, Kolkata, op.cit., pp. 18-19

15. The Calcutta Samaritans & Action Adi, Kolkata, op.cit., pp. 22, 23
16. The Calcutta Samaritans & Action Aid, op.cit., p. 18, & 'Save the Riksha', an article by Whiteleg, John & Williams, Nick posted in Poverty Environment Net, 21.11.2006.

16a. Thomas, T.H., 'Rickshaws in Calcutta', a report, February, 1981, in association with Unnayan, 36/1, Garcha Road, Cal-19, p.37.

17. 'Save the Riksha', jonpardeshi@yahoo.co.in
18. 'Save the Riksha', op. cit.
19. 'Save the Riksha', op. cit.
20. Mainstream, March 27, 1982, 'Hand rickshaws in Calcutta', pp. 27, 28
21. Mainstream, March 27, 1982, op. cit., p. 28
22. Mainstream, March 27, 1982, op. cit. p. 28
23. Ghosal, Soumya Sarkar, www.sahapedia.org, 9th December, 2019.
24. Mainstream, March 27, 1982, op.cit., pp. 28, 29
25. Mainstream, March 27, 1982, op.cit., p. 29.
26. Mainstream, March 27, 1982, op. cit. p. 29.
27. Wheeler, Tony & Anson, Richard 1, 'Chasing Rickshaws', October, 1998.
28. The Calcutta Samaritans & Action Aid, Kolkata, op.cit., pp. 26, 16.

# Chapter III

## Rickshaw Associations and Rickshaw Unions in Calcutta

For the purpose of protecting the interest and promoting the welfare of the handrickshaw owners and handrickshaw pullers, more than one rickshaw associations or Unions have been formed in Calcutta. Out of these associations, the All Bengal Rickshaw Union is still now functioning.

**The All Bengal Rickshaw Union**, having its office at 51, Chittaranjan Avenue was first registered on 27.09.1934. In 1943 the total number of its members were 28871. All its office bearers were rickshaw owners. The list of office bearers on 31.03.1943 is as follows :-

| | | |
|---|---|---|
| President | - | Pratap Singh (44),<br>252, Chittaranjan Avenue. |
| Vice Presidents | - | 1) Golam Gaur (46),<br>40, Ratu Sarkar Lane.<br>2) Lakshmi Kanta Shaw (44),<br>37/2, Mandal Street.<br>3) Khajan Singh (38), 103,<br>Chittaranjan Avenue.<br>4) Bhagwan Das Shaw (38),<br>123/2, Upper Circular<br>Road. |

| | | |
|---|---|---|
| | | 5) Ramani Mohan Banerjee (39), 100/3, Chingrighata Road. |
| | | 6) Sk. Ghani Miah (41), 1/4, Chittaranjan Avenue. |
| | | 7) Pardesi Ram (38), 22, Madan Chatterjee Lane. |
| | | 8) Debi Prosad Shaw (40), 239, Maniktalla Main Road. |
| Treasurer | - | S.C. Varma, 230, Chittaranjan Avenue. |
| General Secretary | - | Khansaheb A. Jabbar (46), 1, Beniapara Lane, a labour leader. |
| Assistant Secretary | - | 1) B.M. Sen (48), 62/3, Beadon Street. |
| | | 2) Md. Zahoor (49), 264, Upper Circular Road. |

Members

There were 23 members in total and all of them were rickshaw owners. The members were as follows :-

1) Mir Wanis Ali (46), 49, Chittaranjan Avenue.
2) Yusuf Mistry (40), 9, Ganipara Lane.
3) Ilahi Buksh (43), 296, Upper Circular Road.
4) Anukul Chandra Roy (56), 15, Madan Boral Street.
5) Debi Prosad De (27), 24/1, Gulu Ostangar Lane.
6) Dahoo Mia (42), 2, Beniapara Lane.
7) Mir Ittahed Hossain (52), 7, St. James Square.
8) Syed Fazul Haq (35), 19/1, Patwar Bagan Lane.
9) Abdul Bani (32), 3, Raja Dinendra Street.

10) Noor Mohammad (41), 3, Ibrahim Road.
11) Behari Singh (45), 17, Deodar Street.
12) Musai Kurmi (52), 80/1, Grey Street.
13) Walayat Hossain (54), 2, Gas Street.
14) Ahmed Din Khan (38), 16, Mitter Lane.
15) Dr. N.C. Datta (34), 89, Dil Khusha Street.
16) B.N. Basu (49), 146, Amherst Street.
17) Abdul Majid (45), 296, Upper Circular Road.
18) Zairuddin (38), 16, Taltola Lane.
19) Nizamuddin (40), 253, Upper Circular Road.
20) Shantilal Patel (42), 40, Chittaranjan Avenue.
21) Tinkori Sarkar (60), Nilmoney Halder Lane, Howrah.
22) Mrs. Saroj Bala Dey (28), Balaram Ghose Street.

It was learnt from the office of the Registrar of Trade Unions, Bengal, that there were three Rickshaw Unions in Calcutta. Besides the Calcutta Rickshaw Mazdoor Union controlled by the C.P.I (Communist Party of India), the other two Unions in Calcutta were Bengal Rickshaw Union and Bengal Rickshaw Mazdoor Union. These two Unions belonged to the white Union[1].

**The All Bengal Rickshaw Union**, established in the year 1934 was formally registered in 1963 under the Trade Unions Act of 1926. At that time this Union had its office at 57-D, Chittaranjan Avenue, Calcutta.

II. According to the Rules and Bye-laws of this Union, the head office of the Union shall be situated in Calcutta with branches in mafussil throughout the province of Bengal, if necessary in the interest of convenient administration[2].

III. The **objects** of this Union are as follows :-

(a) to further a spirit of co-operation amongst the members of the Union by providing a common place of meeting in Caclutta and at outside centres; (b) to promote and protect the interests of the members in all matters, economic, social or political; (c) to feter a spirit of brotherhood and self help among the members; (d) to improve by legal and constitutional means the business or industry in which the members are engaged and to extend the Rickshaw and similar services throughout Calcutta, Howrah and other parts of the province of Bengal; (e) to render assistance to members during trade disputes and to provide for compensation whenever necessary; (f) to make provisions for educational and social benefits of the members; (g) to collect and dissominate such information as may be of use and interest to members; (h) to cooperate with other trade Unions or similar other organisations of employers or workers in India for the purpose of promoting and protecting the Rickshaw business or any other similar industry in all matters, economic, social and political and to act with and help them by legitimate, peaceful and constitutional means and in accordance with the provisions of the Indian Trade Union Act and to affiliate and federate for the said purpose with other Trade Unions and Federations of Trade Unions or similar other organisations or workers in India; (i) to assist in maintaining a periodical published mainly for the purpose of discussing questions affecting employers or workers as such; (j) to raise funds by way of entrance fees, contributions, subscriptions, levies or by such other means as the rules may determine and to do and perform such other lawful acts that may be conducive to or necessary for the fulfilment of the above objects;

(k) to provide for legal assistance to members in matters relating to their trade, whenever required; (l) to run workshops for repairing and manufacturing Rickshaws, the various parts and accessories of Rickshaws, etc. and to import for inland trade all rickshaw goods allied thereto; (m) to remove the grievances of the members and to afford reasonable facilities to the public for popularising the Rickshaw and similar trade, and (n) to standardise the rates of fares and the wages to be paid to pullers or drivers and to provide against sickness, old age, accident and health of members[3].

1. As regards **membership**, every person, not below the age of 18 years, having a rickshaw for hire or a shop dealing with parts or accessories or otherwise engaged in rickshaw trade, shall be eligible for admission to ordinary membership. A candidate for membership shall be duly elected for admission by a majority of votes of the members present at a meeting of the Executive Committee. A candidate may also be admitted on nomination by the President together with any other officer of the Union.

2. Every intending candidate shall sign a declaration form to be provided by the Union. On receiving an application in such form the Secretary shall place it before the Executive Committee and on the applicant being elected as hereinbefore provided, he shall be admitted as a member on payment of all prescribed dues by him[4].

3.(a) A candidate on being elected or nominated as a member, shall pay an entrance fee of 4 annas together with his subscription for the current month.

(b) Subscription for membership shall be payable monthly at the rate mentioned hereinafter.

4. Those ordinary members who pay a sum of Rs.100/- at a time by way subscription shall be called life members of ABRU.

5. Persons, not engaged in or in any way connected to rickshaw business, but have active sympathy with the objects of the Union, may be admitted to the Executive Committee of the Union to act as officers on their election as such by the Executive Committee or by a general meeting. Persons so admitted shall be honorary members of the Union, but their number shall at no time exceed one-half of the total number of officers of the Union for the time being.

6. Any person by paying a lump sum of Rs.500/- or more at a time to the fund of the Union may become a Patron of the Union. A Patron shall enjoy all the rights and privileges of the members[5].

7. The Executive Committee shall have the power to raise a special levy from the ordinary members in any year with the previous approval of the members in a general meeting, annual or extraordinary, provided that any levy made for the purpose of promoting any political or civil interests of members shall not be obligatory on them and that any member unwilling to pay the same shall not be debarred from the privileges of membership of the Union.

8. Every member who fails to pay his subscription for three consecutive months shall forfeit the privileges of membership, but shall be eligible for readmission on payment of all arrear dues.

9. A member shall cease to be a member (a) on his death, (b) on removal of his name under rule 8, (c) on his removal under circumstances hereinafter mentioned, (d) in case of an honorary member, on his ceasing to be a member. The Union shall keep a register of members with such particulars as may be required by the Executive Committee for record and the same shall be open to inspection by its officers and members at any reasonable time during ordinary office hours at its office. The Secretary shall be in charge of the register and shall produce it for inspection when notice of an inspection is given to him[6].

V. **Administration and office**

The management of the Union shall be entrusted to an Executive Committee comprising of 25 members including a President, five Vice-Presidents, a General Secretary, a Joint Secretary and a Treasurer. Unless otherwise arranged by a general meeting, the President shall also act as a Treasurer for the period, as long a suitable person to hold that office if not found[7].

VI. **Executive Committee**

(1) All the officers shall be over 18 years of age; (2) The management and control of the Union shall be vested in the Executive Committee; (3) The members of the Executive Committee shall be elected by the members of the Union at a general meeting; (4) The Executive Committee shall hold at least six meetings in the course of a year and a financial year shall be the official year of the Union; (5) Any item of expenditure over Rs.50/- shall require the sanction of the Executive Committee[8].

VII. **Meeting (ordinary & extraordinary)**

1. The Secretary shall convene the meetings of the Executive Committee as well as the general meetings of the members whenever necessary.
2. Five members shall form a quorum at a meeting of the Executive Committee.
3. The secretary shall call an extra-ordinary meeting of the Executive Committee within a week of the date of the receipt of a requisition signed by at least six members of the Executive Committee, stating the special business rendering an extra-ordinary meeting necessary.
4. At an extra-ordinary meeting only the business included in the notice shall be discussed.
5. Except in emergencies, at least 3 day's notice shall be given of a meeting of the Executive Committee and 7 clear day's notice of general meetings.
6. No question shall be considered by a general meeting of members which has not in the first instance been considered and decided by the Executive Committee or the notice of which has not been given by a member of the Union 48 hours before the time of the meeting.
7. If the Secretary fails to convene a requisition meeting within the time prescribed the requisitionists may themselves call the meeting within a week from the expiry of the prescribed date[9].

VIII. **Vacancies & Removals**

1. Vacancies in the Executive Committee shall be filled up by the remaining members of the

Executive Committee subject to approval by the next general meeting.

2. Every member of the Executive Committee shall vacate the office on the happening of the following events :-

(a) On his failing to attend three consecutive meetings of the Committee, due to illness, accident or any unforeseen matter, the Executive Committee will consider the matter on an application made by the member or by any other member on his or her behalf. The Executive Committee's decision shall be considered as final; (b) On his resigning office by notice in writing to the Secretary of the Union; (c) On his being dead or being found a lunatic or of unsound mind; (d) On his being convicted of moral turpitude in a Court of law; (d) On his being insolvent; (f) If found carrying on activities against the interest of the Union, provided that opportunity shall be given to him to place his case before the Union at a general meeting convened for the purpose and the decision of the Union shall be final[10].

IX. **Powers & Duties of the Executive Committee**

1. Subject to the control and supervision of the general meeting the Executive Committee shall carry on all work conductive to the welfare of the Union and for the attainment of its objects, regularise its income and expenditure. It may frame, rescind, amend or repeal bye rules for its internal management. The Executive Committee shall give due effect to the resolutions of the Annual and other general meetings.

2. It may raise funds in a suitable way whenever necessary and control expenditure.

3. It may appoint as many salaried officers, inspectors, clerks or servants as may be necessary and define their duties, allowances, salaries and privileges and dismiss them or dispense with their services as the occasion arises.
4. It shall submit an Annual Report of the progress of the Union before the members in general meeting together with an audited statement of accounts for the previous year ending on 31st March.
5. It may form sub-committees for special purposes and define their powers.
6. It may appoint or retain Attorneys, Advocates or Pleaders permanently or temporarily to conduct legal work in Courts or offices or for the purpose of legal advice.
7. To institute, conduct, defend, compound or abandon any legal proceeding or grant time for satisfaction or payment of debts or claims due to the Union or may refer any claim or demands by or against the Union to arbitration[11].

X. **Powers & Duties of the President**

1. To preside over all meetings of the Executive Committee and regulate the proceedings of such meetings.
2. To give effect to the rules and regulations made by the Executive Committee.
3. To be an ex-officio member of all the Committees of the Union[12].

XI. **Powers & Duties of the Vice-President**

1. To preside in meetings in the absence of the President and perform his duties.

2. To do all duties delegated to him by the President.

XII. **Duties of the Secretary**

1. Subject to the control and supervision of the Executive Committee the Secretary shall do and transact all business of the Union and shall be in-charge of the office.
2. He shall carry on all correspondence of the Union and sign all letters and papers on behalf of the Union and preserve all such documents, papers, letters and their copies in proper files.
3. He shall maintain a register of members, stock book of articles and account of receipts and expenditure in the ordinary course of business and submit before the Executive Committee every 3 months a statement showing the receipts and disbursements in full and a similar yearly statement before the Annual General Meeting of the Union after the accounts for the year are properly audited.
4. He shall call all meetings, compile reports and minutes of meetings and give effect to the resolutions and direction of the Executive Committee and of the general meeting.
5. He shall give notice and send returns and other documetns required to be given as sent under the Indian Trade Union Act, 1926 to the Registrar of Trade Union, Bengal.
6. He shall distribute works of the Union amongst the staff and exercise control over the management of all works in the interest of the Union.

XIII. **Duties & Powers of the Treasurer**

1. The Treasurer shall be the custodian of the funds and properties of the Union and shall

operate its Bank Accounts and transact all Acts needful therefore.

2. He shall sign or endorse cheque and other financial documents as authorised by the Executive Committee, disburse to the Secretary such sums as shall be granted by the Executive Committee and keep accounts.

3. He may pay Rs.25/- to the Secretary for contigencies without the previous sanction of the Executive Committee[13].

XIV. **Powers & Duties of Assistant Secretary**

To perform all duties delegated to him by the Secretary and to help the Union in the fulfilment of its aims and objects.

XV. **Subscription**

1. Unless otherwise determined by the Executive Committee, the subscription from ordinary owners-members shall be at the following rates :-

| | |
|---|---|
| Holders of 1 to 5 Rickshaws | ...@Rs.4/- per month |
| Holders of 6 to 10 Rickshaws | ...@Rs.8/- per month |
| Holders of 11 to 25 Rickshaws | ...@Re.1/- per month |
| Holders of 26 or over Rickshaws | ...@Rs.2/- per month |

2. The subscription from puller members shall be Rs.2/- per annum payable immediately on enrolment and thereafter within the year for which it is due.

3. The entrance fee shall be monthly 1 to 5 rickshaw owners as Rs.8/- upward Re.1/-.

4. The subscription of owner members to be paid in advance every month.

XVI. **Minutes**

1. The minutes of proceedings of each meeting

shall be entered in a book to be kept in charge of the Secretary and shall be presented for confirmation at the next meeting.

2. The same shall be open to inspection at appointed hours by such and every member or officer.

XVII. **Funds, its Custody, Audit & Purpose**

1. The funds of the Union shall be deposited in a Bank or Post Office Savings Bank as approved by the Executive Committee.

2. The Secretary shall not keep more than Rs.25/- in hand.

3. Every year before the 31st July the Secretary shall arrange to have the accounts audited by the auditor or auditors appointed by the Executive Committee. The appointment of the auditor or auditors for the statutory annual audit and the manner of the said audit shall be governed by the Bengal Trade Union Regulation 1927. The audited accounts shall be placed before the Executive Committee by the Secretary one month previous to presentation before the annual general meeting.

4. Subject to the provisions of Section 15 of the Indian Trade Union Act, 1926, the general funds of the Union shall be spent for all purposes which will promote the objects of the Union as set forth in these rules only except such of them as relate to the political or civic interests of members for payment of the costs of management.

Provided that no part of the general funds shall be applied in carrying any political object or contemplated under class (b) and (h) of Rule

III for which a separate fund may be continued in the manner and within the limitation provided under Section 16 of the said Act.

5. The account books of the Union shall be open to inspection by its officers and members at any time during the normal office hours of the Union[14].

XVIII. **Amendment of Rules**

The rules may be amended, replaced or even added to at any time by the Executive Committee provided that such amendment, replacement or addition shall require the approval of a general meeting held for the purpose within three weeks from the date of its being passed by the Executive Committee and shall require to be duly registered under the Indian Trade Union Act, 1926.

XIX. **General Meeting (Annual)**

1. The Annual General Meeting of the Union shall be held ordinarily in the month of June to transact the following business.

(a) to adopt the report of work done by the Union and the statement of accounts duly audited by the appointed Auditor relating to the previous year ending 31st March.

(b) To elect office bearers and an Executive Committee of the Union for the current year.

(c) To sanction the budget for the current year.

(d) To transact any other business brought by the Secretary.

2. The quorum shall be at least one-fifth of the total number of members of the Union.

XX. **Notice** – A fortnight's notice shall be given to members of the Annual General Meeting but

Extra-ordinary General Meeting may be called by the Secretary or requisitionist on three days' notice.

XXI. **R.B. Licence**

A fee of Rs.1/8/- shall be charged from each rickshaw bearer for the purpose of getting him a licence.

XXII. **Dissolution**

The Union shall not be dissolved except by a majority of three-fourth votes of the members present at a general meeting especially called for the purpose provided that the votes cast shall not be less than three-fifth of the total number of members of the Union after dissolution of funds shall be distributed amongst the members in accordance with a resolution passed at such meeting.

Provided that the balance of funds at the credit of the Union at the time of dissolution shall not be disposed of until the dissolution has been duly registered under the Indian Trade Union Act, 1926 and an acknowledgement of registry received from the Registrar[15].

Subsequently the office of the All Bengal Rickshaw Union was shifted to 51, Chittaranjan Avenue, Calcutta – 700012.

As per the auditor's Report on the accounts of the Union for the year ended on 31st December, 1998, the income of the Union fell far short of the total expenditure and there was no cash in hand of the General Secretary or Treasurer as on 31st December, 1998. The matured amount of the Fixed Deposits of Rs.1,05,270/- stood at Rs.13,3100/- and the entire amount was reinvested.[16]

The Presidents and General Secretaries from the year 1960 to 2000 were as follows :-

| Year | Presidents | General Secretaries |
|---|---|---|
| 1960 | Sri Ramoni Mohan Banerjee | A. Jabbar |
| 1961 | Sri Ram Krishna Mukherjee | A. Jabbar |
| 1962 | Sri Pardeshi Ram | A. Jabbar |
| 1963 | Sri S.K. Sengupta | A. Jabbar |
| 1964 | Sri Thakur Singh | A. Jabbar |
| 1965 | Sri S.L. Hemmady | A. Jabbar |
| 1966 | Sri S.L. Hemmady | A. Jabbar |
| 1967 | Sri S.L. Hemmady | A. Jabbar |
| 1968 | Sri Benoy Kr. Das | A. Jabbar |
| 1969 | Sri B.K. Das | A. Jabbar |
| 1970 | Sri B.K. Das | A. Jabbar |
| 1971 | Sri Motilal Ghosal | A. Jabbar |
| 1972 | Sri Motilal Ghosal | A. Jabbar |
| 1973 | Sri Motilal Ghosal | B.M. Sen |
| 1974 | No record | |
| 1975 | Sri M.S. Zoha, M.L.A. | B.M. Sen |
| 1976 | Sri M.S. Zoha, M.L.A. | B.M. Sen |
| 1977 | Sri M.S. Zoha, M.L.A. | B.M. Sen |
| 1978 | Sri M.S. Zoha, M.L.A. | B.M. Sen |
| 1979 | Jb. Kalimuddin Shams Hon'ble Deputy Speaker, West Bengal Legislative Assembly | Samir Chandra Dutta |
| 1980 | -do- | Ashok Kr. Sharma |
| 1981 | -do- | Ashok Kr. Sharma |
| 1982 | Sri Kalimuddin Shams | Ashok Kr. Sharma |
| 1983 | Sri Kalimuddin Shams | Ashok Kr. Sharma |
| 1984 | Sri Kalimuddin Shams | Ashok Kr. Sharma |

| | | |
|---|---|---|
| 1985 | Sri Kalimuddin Shams | Ashok Kr. Sharma |
| 1986 | Sri Kalimuddin Shams | Sanat Kr. Banerjee |
| 1987 | Sri Somen Mitra, M.L.A. | Jb. Abdul Wahab |
| 1988 | Sri Somen Mitra, M.L.A. | Jb. Abdul Wahab |
| 1989 | Sri Somen Mitra, M.L.A. | Jb. Abdul Wahab |
| 1990 | Sri Somen Mitra, M.L.A. | Sanat Kr. Banerjee |
| 1991 | Sri Somen Mitra, M.L.A. | Sanat Kr. Banerjee |
| 1992 | Sri Somen Mitra, M.L.A. | Sanat Kr. Banerjee |
| 1993 | Sri Somen Mitra, M.L.A. | Abdul Wahab |
| 1994 | Sri Somen Mitra, M.L.A. | Abdul Wahab |
| 1995 | Sri Somen Mitra, M.L.A. | Abdul Wahab |
| 1996 | Sri Somen Mitra, M.L.A. | Abdul Wahab |
| 1997 | Sri Somen Mitra, M.L.A. | Mr. Mukhtar Ali (Acting General Secretary) |
| 1998 | Sri Somen Mitra, President & Sri Sultan Ahmed, M.L.A., Working President | Mr. Mukhtar Ali (Acting General Secretary) |
| 1999 | Sri Somen Mitra, President & Sri Sultan Ahmed, M.L.A., working President | Mr. Mukhtar Ali (Acting General Secretary) |
| 2000 | Sri Somen Mitra, President & Sri Sultan Ahmed, M.L.A., working President | Mr. Mukhtar Ali (Acting General Secretary[17]) |
| 2001 | Sri Somen Mitra, President & Jb. Sultan Ahmed, M.L.A., working President | Jb. Mukhtar Ali (General Secretary) |

As per the Auditor's Report dated 7th March, 2001, the income of the All Bengal Rickshaw Union fell far short of expenditure. Increase of annual subscription of the owners from September, 2000 might show some improvement of income in the next year, provided expenses were controlled. There was no cash in hand of the General Secretary or Treasurer at the close of business on 31st December, 2000. The amount of fixed deposit stood at Rs.1,61,900/- as on 31st December, 2000 as against Rs.1,49,960/- at the close of the previous year[18].

## Activities of ABRU

The Union office used to handle all problems faced by the rickshawpullers in case of violation of traffic signal or in case of keeping the rickshaw in the no parking zone or in case of the rickshawpuller carrying stolen articles such as iron pieces or other stolen articles in his rickshaw without having any knowledge about the same. In such cases of illegal activities when the police caught the puller and lodged a case against him, the Union people used to rescue the puller by visiting the police station, handling the case and paying a fine. Four persons were employed in the Union who dealt with these problems of the pullers.

Now there are around 32 members in the Executive Committee of ABRU and these members are all rickshaw owners, of whom 15 are muslims and 15 are hindus, out of which 7/8 are Bengalees. Since 1991 till 2000 an alopathic doctor used to sit in the Union office from 10-00 a.m. to 5-00 p.m. for attending to the medical need of the rickshawpullers. The Union office used to provide medicine and money to the ailing rickshawpullers. During the epidemic of Covid in 2020-21 the ABRU provided food and medical aid to the rickshawpullers. But since 2006 the Union had stopped its activities as the rickshaw trade is on the decline due to non-issuance of licence to the rickshawpullers and the rickshaw owners. No new generation of rickshawpullers are now forthcoming.

Most of the old rickshaw pullers are dead or have gone home forever. Their children are now doing alternative work to earn an income and they are no longer interested in this rickshaw business[19].

Kishan Deo Yadav, a rickshaw owner and an Executive Committee member of ABRU informs us that in the 1970s a doctor used to sit in the Union's Office to cater to the medical need of the pullers[20].

At present the office bearers of ABRU are as follows :-

Mohammad Ishaq, President
Kashinath Paul, Vice President
Mukhtar Ali, General Secretary
and Anirban Dutta, Treasurer.

## Calcutta Rickshaw Association

Some rickshaw owners of Calcutta considering the various difficulties in carrying on the rickshaw business in Calcutta and in the suburbs met together in a meeting at 62/3, Beadon Street, Calcutta on 15th October, 1939 and unanimously passed the following resolution with Mr. Bepin Mohan Sen in the chair :-

"Resolved that to improve the rickshaw business in general in Calcutta and its suburbs, an association be formed and registered under the Indian Trade Union Act, 1926 and also that the following persons viz : (1) Debi Prasad Shaw, (2) Babulal Bania, (3) Jatindranath Sen, (4) Jatindranath Roy Chowdhury, (5) Bepin Mohan Sen, (6) Santi Lal Patel and (7) Gobinda Chandra Chanda be authorised to promote and get registered the desired Association. The office-bears of the Calcutta Rickshaw Association were as follows :-

President - Debi Prosad Shaw
Vice-President - Babu Lal Bania
Jatindra Nath Roy Chowdhury

| | |
|---|---|
| Secretary - | Dr. Jatindranath Sen |
| Assistant Secretaries - | Bipin Mohan Sen<br>Gopal Chandra Chanda |
| Treasurer - | Santi Lal Patel |
| Ordinary Members - | Chotey Lal Patel<br>Belait Hossain<br>Isuf Mia<br>Ramjan, Abdul Mia,<br>Md. Jalil[21]. |

**Rules for the Calcutta Rickshaw Association**

1. The association is a combination of businessmen engaged in Rickshaw business in Calcutta and it shall be called "The Calcutta Rickshaw Association".
2. The head office of the association shall be in Calcutta.
3. The objects for which the Association is established are :-

   (a) To promote, organize and improve the rickshaw business in general in Calcutta and suburbs and to strive to bring together the rickshaw owners as well as the rickshaw bearers of Calcutta in order to effect a concerted action for the upkeep and maintenance of their common interest.

   (b) To make efforts of curtailing the present heavy expenditure of securing Rickshaw bearers' licence by prayers and appeals through proper channel.

   (c) To organize the rickshaw bearers in such a way that they may not put to lose and harass the owners by wilful practices of securing licence through the money and efforts of one owner and subsequently serving another etc.

(d) To run workshops and factories for repairing and manufacturing the rickshaw parts and accessories so that the running cost of purchasing foreign made parts and accessories may be considerably reduced.

(e) To start and maintain training school for imparting necessary instructions to the prospective rickshaw bearers before they are sent up for licence.

(f) To enter into any agreement or arrangement with the local government that they seem expedient.

(g) To do or undertake such other things as are incidental or as may be deemed expedient for the attainment of any of the above objects of the Association.

4. Any person or persons owning a Rickshaw and engaged in the Rickshaw business in Calcutta shall be eligible for admission as ordinary members of the Association.

5. In case of a joint ownership of the same Rickshaw or Rickshaws, the joint owners shall duly authorise any of them to represent himself as a member of the Association.

6. Every ordinary member shall pay a monthly subscription of not less than 4 annas and not more than one rupee payable immediately on enrolment and thereafter by the end of the month for which it is due.

7. No member shall remain a member if he is in arrears with his subscriptions for 6 months and does not clear his dues by the end of the $6^{th}$ month.

8. Persons not eligible for admission as ordinary members under Rule 4 may be admitted as

honorary members to serve the Executive Committee of the association upto a total of half of the total number of members of the Executive body.

9. All the members of the Executive Committee for the time being shall retire from office at the first annual general meeting and in every subsequent year. All members of the Executive Committee shall be elected at the annual general meeting of the Association.

10. Retiring members of the Executive Committee shall be eligible for re-election.

11. Any member, ordinary or honorary is eligible for election as a member of the Executive Committee.

12. The President of the Association shall usually preside over the meetings of the Executive Committee. But if the President is absent at any meeting, the members present shall choose some one of them to be the Chairman of the meeting.

13. The Association shall have a general fund which shall include all income from subscriptions from members, donations and other miscellaneous sources. All expenses of the association including salaries and allowances to offices shall be met from the general fund.

14. All money belonging to the Association shall be in the custody of the Treasurer, provided all sums except those immediately required shall be deposited in a bank or banks approved by the Executive Committee.

15. The remuneration of the Secretary shall be a monthly allowance of Rs.25/- from the date of incorporation of the Association.

16. The Secretary shall cause proper books of accounts to be kept which shall be entered true and complete accounts of the income and expenditure of the Association.
17. The Secretary shall also maintain a register of members, name, age, address and such other particulars as may be considered necessary concerning each member, including an honorary member.
18. The Executive Committee may take disciplinary action against any member of the association and may fine, suspend membership and forfeit the rights and benefits for a certain period or altogether remove from the Association. Such a member if he is found guilty of any activity hostile to the interests of the association of any behavior or corrupt practices shall face disciplinary action from the Executive Committee.
19. The Union shall not be dissolved except by the decision of the majority of members assembled at a meeting specially called for the purpose. The quorum for the meeting shall be two third of the total number of members of the Association for the time being. This meeting shall decide in what manner the funds of the Association, after dissolution, if any, shall be disposed of[22].

There is no office for the Calcutta Rickshaw Association although it has been registered to be at 167/1, Manicktolla Street. The Secretary was available at 9, Gora Chand Bose Road and the Assistant Secretary, Bepin Mohan Sen was available at 62/3, Beadon Street.

The reason behind starting this Association is that Abdul Jabbar with Suresh Chandra Varma,

Nathuni Shaw and Golam Gaus had been conducting the affairs of the All Bengal Rickshaw Union most wilfully and unconstitutionally. They had been totally ignoring the Executive Body and the general members in respect of accounts, appointments and dismissal of officers of the Union, keeping off all the meetings and in all other matters which are expressly intended by the rules of the Union to be done only with the sanction of the Executive Committee or in a general meeting. J.N. Sen assisted by Bepin Mohan Sen started this Association and it is a white Union but it is parallel to All Bengal Rickshaw Unioin (as per the report of Brojo Lal Roy, Sub-Inspector, Special Branch, 9/12/39)[23].

The Calcutta Rickshaw Association was registered under the Trade Union Act, 1926, by the Labour Commissioner on 29.11.1939. All the Committee members of the Calcutta Rickshaw Association were rich and influential rickshaw owners and they were all previously members of All Bengal Rickshaw Union (1) Golam Ghaush, living with his family at 40, Rottu Sircar Lane, was the owner of 70 rickshaws, (2) Khan Sahib Abdul Jabbar, was the General Secretary of All Bengal Rickshaw Union and a labour organiser, (3) Babu Suresh Chandra Varma, living with his family at 230, Central Avenue, was the owner of 70 rickshaws, (4) Nathuni Shaw, living with his family at 147, Keshab Sen Street, was the owner of 150 rickshaws[24].

At a meeting of the Calcutta Docker's Union held at the foot of the Ochterlony Monument on 23.03.1940, Khan Sahib Khan Jabbar announced that no rickshaw would ply for hire on 28.03.1940 to enable all pullers and owners to cast their votes in the Corporation election[25].

According to the report of B. Roy Choudhury dated 28.05.1944 the rickshaw owners charged too much from the pullers. Besides this the Police realised illegal gratification from them and prosecuted them. The ration they got was quite inadequate to maintain themselves[26].

**The Bengal Rickshaw Mazdoor Union** came into existence on 20th September, 1943 and had on its roll 50 members. It had its office at 39/1, Hatibagan Road, Calcutta and this Union was registered on 25.05.1944. Its office bearers were as follows :-

| | |
|---|---|
| President - | K.C. Roychoudhury (50 years), 44, Hindustan Park. |
| Vice President - | Abdul Hamid Khan (26 years), 18, Gora Chand Lane- Fitter. |
| Joint Secretary - | 1. Surjoog Ram Mehra (32 years), 34, Christopher Road, a blacksmith |
| | 2. Sk. Solrati Miah (38 years), 34A, Collin Street, a rickshawpuller |
| Treasurer - | Dhanaram Paswan (28 years), 51, Dr. Suresh Sankar Road, a blacksmith |

The Executive Committee members of this Union were as follows :-

(1) Algoo Ram (35), 23, Christopher Road, a cobbler

(2) Ziamuddin Khan (34), 29, Dr. S. Sarkar Road, a tailor

(3) Jogi Ram Koray (32), 3, Kamandanga Road, a rickshawpuller

(4) Barsati Ram Chauth (26), 4, Kamandanga Road, a rickshaw puller.

(5) Wazi Hassan (34), 30, Elliot Lane, a mechanic

(6) Bhola Thakur (28), 25, Christopher Road, a carpenter

(7) Abdul Sattar (23), 50/1, Dr. Suresh Sankar Road, a tailor

(8) Mohiuddin (25), 50/1, Dr. Suresh Sankar Road, a painter

(9) Abdul Karim (32), 13, Mc. Leod Street, a painter[27].

There was another organisation of handrickshaw pullers named as **Calcutta Rickshaw Chalak Panchayat** having its office at 4, Bhukailash Road, Khidderpore, Calcutta – 700023. Noor Ahmed was the President and Ganapati Jha was the General Secretary of this Panchayat. On 19th September, 1996 this Panchayat called a strike of the rickshaw pullers.

**The Calcutta Rickshaw Mazdoor Union** (registered No.550) of 249, Bowbazar Street approached the Commissioner of Police for recognition of their claim to represent rickshawpullers as against the existing All Bengal Rickshaw Union. In reply to a letter dated 16.08.1944 vide Memo No. M.V. 11662 H.C.B. File No. G100(1) sent by the Calcutta Public Vehicles Department at 38, Beltolla Road, to Barnes, Esqr. I.P.J.P., Deputy Commissioner of Police, Special Branch, Calcutta, enquiring about the Calcutta Rickshaw Mazdoor Union, it was found that this Union had its office at 249, Bowbazar Street, B.K. Roy Choudhury, Sub-Inspector, Calcutta Police, Special Branch, in his report on the Calcutta Rickshaw Mazdoor Union, stated that this Union came into existence on 24.04.1944 and had on its roll 259 members on 15.05.1944. This Union was registered on 13.07.1944[28].

The office bearers of the Calcutta Rickshaw

Mazdoor Union were :

| | |
|---|---|
| President – | Md. Ismail (32), Councillor of Corporation of Calcutta; |
| Vice-President – | (1) Kamalji (30), 98, Harrison Road, trade unionist; |
| | (2) Bejoy Kumar Singh (30), 55, Tarak Pramanick Road, a rickshawpuller. |
| General Secretary - | Mihir Bose (23), 249, Bowbazar Street, a trade unionist. |
| Assistant Secretary - | (1) Nato Bhattacharjee (23), a trade unionist. |
| | (2) Ajit Sinha (25), 13/2A, Russa Road, a trade unionist. |
| Treasurer - | Pradyot Nag (24), 249, Bowbazar Street, a trade unionist. |

There were 19 members in total in the Executive Committee of this Union and all these members were rickshaw pullers. They were namely as follows :-

(1) Raghunandan Rao (32), 133, Upper Circular Road

(2) Mangal Mia (55), 244, Upper Circular Road

(3) Jilaki Shaw (33), 15, Madan Baral Lane

(4) Mukta Routh (40), 15, Madan Baral Lane

(5) Suklal Dusad (30), Hiralal Banerjee Lane

(6) Jinat Ali (35), 7, Malanga Lane

(7) Ram Prosad (40), 13, Suterkin Street

(8) Chetan Paswan (34), 15, Baisnab Sett 1st Lane

(9) Sk. Hanif (30), 11, Central Avenue

(10) Jagroo Molla (50), 16/1, Ultadingi Road

(11) Rasul Mia (26), 10A, Lalit Mitra Lane

(12) Bodhan Mahato (30), 15, Mohan Bagan Lane
(13) Singheswar (22), 5, Andul Raj Road
(14) Radha Kisan (30), 14/4, Grove Lane
(15) Bathu (27), 88A, Rashbehari Avenue
(16) Dillu (40), 14, Jogesh Mitra Road
(17) Sitaram (24), 25/4, Chakraberia Road
(18) Jogi Kewat (28), 9, Dr. Rajendra Road
(19) Dinal (24), 4, Govinda Addi Road[29].

## Activities of the Calcutta Rickshaw Mazdoor Union

During the period from September to December, 1945 the Calcutta Rickshaw Mazdoor Union affiliated to CPI held several meetings of the rickshaw pullers in Calcutta. On 01.09.1945 Moh. Ismail led a deputation of about 30 strikers to the Labour Commissioner and placed their demands for a settlement. The Labour Commissioner sent for representatives of the All Bengal Rickshaw Union and accordingly 4 representatives of the Union participated in the settlement talks. On the recommendation of the Additional Labour Commissioner a provisional settlement was accepted by the representatives of the pullers and owners. On 07.09.1945 at a meeting of 700 rickshawpullers at Wellington Square with Moh. Ismail as the President resolutions were passed—

condemning the rickshaw owners for flouting the terms of settlement arrived on 01.09.1945 and resenting their demand of depositing hiring charges at an increased of Rs.1/8 and Rs.1-4-0 for the new and old rickshaws against the settled rates of Rs.1/2, urging the Public Vehicles Department to intervene and take action against the owners who were not letting their rickshaws on hire at the settled rates and seeking redress of police on the pullers from the Commissioner of Police[30].

Again on 12.09.1945 at Beadon Square another meeting was held by the Calcutta Rickshaw Mazdoor Union with Md. Ismail as the President. The speakers namely Balgovind Mahato, Ram Lakshman Mahato, Fauzi Dasad, S. Mitra and the President urged the rickshaw pullers to unite for compelling the owners to abide by the terms of the settlement and for redress of their own grievances. Resolutions were passed condemning the rickshaw owners for not abiding by the terms of the settlement and urging the Labour Commissioner and the P.V.D. to intervene for the redress of their genuine grievances and urging the pullers to unite and fight against all repressions of the owners.

Two meetings were held one on 14.09.1945 and the other on 15.09.1945 at Mohammad Ali Park and at the Children's Park respectively. The speakers namely the President Gour Babu, Ganga Rao, Bhola Bhai, Bhabani Sen and Sisir Mitra urged the pullers to unite and stick to the terms of the settlement. They also urged for the formation of committees in each khatal and the enrolment of as many members of the Union as possible on payment of a monthly subscription of 4 annas. At the meeting on 15.09.1945, Pranab Kumar Ghosh presided and Bhabani Roy Choudhuri announced that a committee of rickshaw pullers will be formed soon to look after their interests[31].

Another meeting was held on 07.10.1945 by Calcutta Rickshaw Mazdoor Union on the same issue of the owners flouting the terms of the settlement made by the Labour Commissioner. President Abdul Razzak, Saral Kumar Agnihotri, Ajodhya Prasad, Moh. Din and many others were the speakers in this meeting[32].

On 28.11.1945, the rickshaw pullers of south Calcutta went on strike protesting against the present exhorbitant rate of payment for each rickshaw to the owners daily. In this meeting of 800 rickshawpullers held at Hazra Park it was pointed out that the rate of payment of Rs.2-4-0 per day for each rickshaw to the owners was excessive in comparison to pre-war rate. On 29.11.1945 in the morning there was a partial strike of the rickshawpullers of north Calcutta and central Calcutta. On 30.11.1945 the rickshawpullers actually went on a complete strike and also held a meeting at Wellington Square wherein Moh. Ismail denounced the owners for charging deposits at higher rates from the pullers. He urged the strikers to continue the strike till their demands were fulfilled and also urged the strikers to march in procession all over Calcutta to show to the public the unity of the rickshaw pullers. On 30.11.1945 around 14-00 hours 150 rickshaw pullers assembled in Hazra Park and left in a procession along Russa Road, Beltola Road and Lansdowne Road. Another procession of about 100 rickshaw pullers marched along Ramesh Mitra Road. Both processions carried the usual Communist flags and shouted slogans[33].

On 01.12.1945 at a meeting of 2,500 rickshaw pullers held by the Calcutta Rickshaw Mazdur Union at Wellington Square, with Rezzaque and later Md. Ismail as the Presidents, the high deposits demanded by the rickshaw owners for hiring of rickshaws was discussed B.L. Govind spoke in this meeting that the police authorities were partly responsible for the unsatisfactory position of the rickshaw pullers inasmuch as there were only 6000 licensed rickshaws but there were more than 40,000 licensed pullers. There was thus superfluity of workmen whom the owners could play off one against the other. Md. Ismail also accused the police and the owners of inhuman and brutal treatment of the rickshaw pullers. He stated that there were 6,000 rickshaws and 1 lakh of pullers and for this the Police Vehicle Department should be held responsible. After the meeting ended, about 2,000 rickshaw pullers formed a procession and paraded Ganesh Avenue, Chittaranjan Avenue, Chowringhee, Ashutosh Mukherjee Road and Russa Road and dispersed at Kalighat Park[34].

On 02.12.1945 at a meeting of 1,500 rickshaw pullers at Wellington Square with Dhiren Mazumdar (C.P.I.) in the Chair, resolutions were passed :-

reiterating their decision to continue their strike until all their demands were fulfilled, drawing the attention of the National Press and the citizens of Calcutta to the grievances of the rickshaw pullers and urging the Labour Commissioner to settle the dispute as early as possible. After this meeting a procession of 1,500 pullers went to the Calcutta Rickshaw Workers Union's office at 249, Bowbazar Street through Mission Row and Chittaranjan Avenue. The All Bengal Rickshaw Union (ABRU) (white) affiliated to the Bengal National Chamber/ Labour was not in favour of the present strike and persistently tried to avert it but failed because of the adament attitude of the Calcutta Rickshaw Majdur Union (C.P.I.) which was bent upon increasing their hold on the rickshaw pullers by calling a strike. The ABRU convened a meeting of rickshaw owners and representatives of rickshaw pullers on 02.12.1945 at this office with Khan Sahab

Abdul Jabbar as President and decided that the rickshaw pullers would resume work from 03.12.1945 at the agreed rate of Re.1 & Re.1/2 for on old rickshaw and a new rickshaw per shift respectively[35].

The Calcutta Rickshaw Mazdoor Union held several meetings of the pullers on 04.12.1945, 07.12.1945, 08.12.1945, 09.12.1945, 12.12.1945, 13.12.1945 and 14.12.1945 at Wellington Square with Khet Narain Missir and Md. Ismail as the Presidents in these meetings. The main issue of discussion in all these meetings was to urge the rickshaw pullers to continue their strike till their legitimate demands were fulfilled, to unite under the Union, to condemn the rickshaw owners and the police for jointly coercing the strikers to resume work. At a meeting of 2,000 pullers, held on 14.12.1945 at Wellington Square, Md. Ismail announced that the owners had given their terms of settlement viz. the owners would reduce the deposit (Jama) from Rs.1/2/- & Re.1/- to Re.1/- and 14 annas for new and old rickshaws respectively, bear the expenses of petty cases concerning their rickshaws, pay for the oil for rickshaw lights and make arrangement for medical treatment of rickshaw pullers. The most important result of the strike was that the issue of new licence had been stopped. The rickshaw pullers' strike was called off by the Calcutta Rickshaw Mazdoor Union at its meeting held on 14.12.1945[36].

The Additional Labour Commissioner of Bengal, S.A.E.B. Murshedi vide a letter No.6151-L.C. dated 14.12.1945 informed the Secretary, Calcutta Rickshaw Mazdoor Union having its office at 249, Bowbazar Street, Calcutta, that after his discussion with the representatives of the owners nominated by the All Bengal Rickshaw Union (ABRU) regarding the demands put forward by the representatives of the Calcutta Rickshaw Mazdoor Union, the reduction of 'Jama' as decided by the owners was just and adequate. The Addl. Labour Commissioner further informed that the owners stated to him that they had always been bearing the maintenance cost of rickshaws but they never paid for the oil of the lamps kept underneath the rickshaw. The decision of the Commissioner of Police was that the rickshaw would not be allowed to loiter and tout for hire on the Chowringhee Road. The ABRU asserted that the owners always paid fines for petty cases in case of obstruction of traffic but no fines were imposed on pullers for plying without light at night or for cases like theft[37].

The All Bengal Rickshaw Union (ABRU) asserted before the Addl. Labour Commissioner, Bengal that necessary medicines were supplied free to the rickshawpullers from two of their dispensaries, one situated in their head office at Chittaranjan Avenue and the other in Ward No.VI.

Outlines of a scheme for restricting issue of licences was drawn up by S.A.E.B. Murshedi, Addl. Labour Commissioner and agreed by the representatives of both parties (pullers & owners) and the police. Under this scheme temporary licence would not be issued unless the number of pullers present and available for work in Calcutta on any day was less than 24,000 i.e. 4 times the number of rickshaws. As regards the issue of payment of passage money to home and back for the pullers once a year by the owner was not accepted by the owners and also not recommended by the office of the Labour Commissioner, Bengal at 8, Clive Street, Clive Bldgs., Calcutta. The rickshaw owners also refused to recognize the Calcutta Rickshaw Mazdoor Union[38].

On 18.12.1945, Md. Ismail as President of Calcutta Rickshaw Mazdur Union and other speakers urged the rickshawpullers to join this Union and to raise a fund of Rs.900/- for the development of the Union. They further stressed the need for enlisting at least 2000 volunteers in the Union to fight against the oppression of the owners. They also urged the pullers to follow the lead of the C.P.I.

On the issue of reduction of the high rate of deposit realised by the owners, several strikes were called, one on 17.04.1946 by around 200 rickshawpullers at Kidderpore and the other on 22.09.1947 at the Children's Park (behind Park Circus Tram Depot). The owners having fixed the deposit money at a flat rate of 13 annas per diem for both new and old rickshaw, the strike was called off on 19.04.1946 at Kidderpore. In Park Circus area the strike was called off on 23.09.1947 where the owners agreed to receive 12 annas and 8 annas for day and night shifts respectively as deposit (jama) from the pullers[39].

### Report of Dr. T.H. Thomas :

According to the report of Dr. T.H. Thomas of Warwick University, U.K. who made a research study on this rickshaws in Calcutta in 1981, there are two rickshaw associations in Calcutta, one is All Bengal Rickshaw Union founded in 1939 and the other is the Rickshaw Owners' Association founded in 1978. The ABRU represents the interest of over 2000 owners including lapsed membership according to the register of members maintained by the office bearers of ABRU in November, 1980. This number is uncertain as the number of members obtained from a discussion with ABRU in November, 1980, was 1300 only. The ROA (Rickshaw Owners' Association) represents the interest of 2200 owners of rickshaws which were until 1980, licenced in municipalities around Calcutta (Baranagar, South Dum Dum, Rajpur). These vehicles, to our knowledge had Bengal licences. In 1980 the municipalities stopped renewal of licences following a circular from the State Government[40].

According to Dr. Thomas the ABRU was founded to resist the implementation of the provisions of the West Bengal Hackney Carriage Act, 1919 amended in 1939 by acting as a political pressure group. The ABRU also assists its member owners in the running of their fleets by handling certain aspects of vehicles and puller licence applications. In February, 1981, the President of ABRU (who was also the Deputy Speaker of the Legislative Assembly) was reported as saying that the ABRU was willing to help "to remove unauthorized rickshaws from the city streets". (The Statesman, 9th February, 1981). Thus the line between the legal and illicit parts of the trade is therefore not a sharp one[41].

### Rally and Strike called by ABRU and other Unions in the 1990s and after 2000.

It is evident from a letter dated 19th September, 1996 sent by President Noor Ahmed and General Secretary Ganapati Jha of Calcutta Rickshaw Chalak Panchayat to Mr. Subhas Chakravarty, the then Minister of Transport & Sports, Government of West Bengal, that their Union had called all handrickshaw pullers and owners to observe a day of token strike on 19th September, 1996 and to hold a mass rally at the Esplanade East to protest against the Government's policy of banning hand pulled rickshaws. Sri George Fernandes, Sri Nitesh

Kumar and Sri Ananda Mohan Singh all M.Ps along with local trade Union leaders addressed this rally. The Calcutta Rickshaw Chalak Panchayat had its office at 4, Bhukailash Road (Kidderpore), Calcutta – 700023 and it was a registered Union and affiliated to Hind Mazdoor Kisan Panhayat[42].

The All Bengal Rickshaw Union, in protest against the Transport Minister's decision to stop plying of handpulled rickshaws in the city of Calcutta after 31st December, 1996, called all the rickshaw pullers and owners to join in a rally at Sidhu Kanu Dahar (Esplanade East) on 30th September, 1996 at 1-00 p.m. Mr. Abdul Wahab, General Secretary of ABRU invited Sm. Mamata Banerjee, the then M.P. for her kind participation in the said rally for encouraging the rickshaw pullers and owners in their struggle for existence[43].

It is interesting to note that a ***Racing Rally of hand pulled Rickshaws*** was held on 30.01.2005 in which 25 to 30 hand rickshaw pullers participated. The venue of this programme was at Ram Lilla Park, Middle Road, Kolkata – 700011. The Rally was named as *Rickshaw Fellowship Race.*

On 25th June, 2011, the ***Hath Rickshaw Rozgar Bachao Manch*** held a convention at Moulali Yuba Kendra to discuss the issue of rehabilitation package for the rickshaw pullers. Though the former Chief Minister Buddhadeb Bhattacharjee announced a rehabilitation package for rickshaw pullers at a press conference on 15th August 2005, subsequently the Kolkata Municipal Corporation stopped issuing licence to the rickshawpullers and the city police began to seize the rickshaws on the plea that they were illegally plying on the road. In the past six years since 2005 no rehabilitation package was prepared by the State Government.

False cases were levelled against those who failed to bribe the police, alleged the aggrieved rickshawpullers. Mr. Mukhtar Ali, convener of the Hath Rickshaw Rozgar Bachao Manch said that he had given a representation to the former Chief Minister and Mayor Mr. Bikash Ranjan Bhattacharya to announce the rehabilitation package and till the package was announced, rickshaws should be allowed to ply. But they refused to listen. He said that rickshaws would ply in the city despite the ban till rehabilitation package was announced as "it was wrong to stop someone from earning his livelihood without making proper arrangement by alternative means[44]. In this convention the rickshawpullers urged the State Government for preservation of the hand pulled rickshaw as it is a heritage and part of the city's history. With the State Government's proposal to introduce walk tourism in north Calcutta, rickshaws would be the ideal mode of transport to carry tourists to visit important houses in lanes and by-lanes. This convention was attended by social activist Mrs. Anuradha Talwar and the convener of Hath Rickshaw Rozgar Bachao Manch, Mr. Mukhtar Ali, who protested against the "black bill" enacted by the Left Front Government in 2006 to abolish rickshaws from the city. Mrs. Talwar said the State Government had said that rickshaws tarnish the image of the city as it is inhuman that people are being carried by their fellow men. But she said there is nothing wrong in this as long as they are earning a respectable livelihood. She further said that rickshaws may be turned into a major tourist attraction to upgrade the condition of the rickshawpullers. She also suggested that as it is zero pollution transportation, the Government must encourage this means of transport in lanes and by-lanes of Calcutta. Rickshawpullers also alleged that police often harassed them and demanded money from them without any rhyme or reason[45]. Social activist, Ms. Anuradha Talwar said that certain areas should be declared out of bounds for motor transport with only rickshaws allowed to ply. This move will also help in lessening pollution. She further said "the rickshaw pullers are a symbol of the city, so a limited number of the rickshaw could be kept as tourist attraction". She also suggested that the rehab measures should put major emphasis on the pullers than the rickshaw owners and the pullers be provided with cycle rickshaws[46].

The All Bengal Rickshaw Union (ABRU) decided to meet Miss Mamata Banerjee since she became the Chief Minister of West Bengal, pinning their hopes of reviving their livelihood on the Chief Minister whom they hail as the voice of the poor and oppressed. Mr. Mukhtar Ali, convener, ABRU said, "Amid all despair and darkness Didi is our only hope. We will meet Didi with our grievances and ask her to ban this black law". Mr. Ali further said, "we are plying without licence for which the police often confiscate our rickshaws. We have to pay Rs.80/- as fine which is often our daily earning". In the year 2011 around 17,000 pullers were plying 6,000 odd rickshaws in the central and southern parts of the metropolis[47].

At present, save and except the All Bengal Rickshaw Union (ABRU) having its office at premises No.51, Chittaranjan Avenue, Calcutta-12, 1st floor, all other associations and unions of the handrickshaw owners and pullers, namely the Calcutta Rickshaw Association, the Bengal Rickshaw Mazdoor Union, the Calcutta Rickshaw

Mazdoor Union and Calcutta Rickshaw Chalak Panchayet have closed down. Under the able guidance and initiative of Mr. Mukhtar Ali, the General Secretary of ABRU, the All Bengal Rickshaw Union is still operating in full force and the office bearers and members of this Union have taken up the cause of the handrickshaw pullers and owners in the matter of banning of handrickshaw in Calcutta and the vital issue of rehabilitation of the rickshawpullers and owners by the state government. Mr. Mukhtar Ali together with his team of members of ABRU have been continuously and tirelessly agitating for the cause of rehabilitation of the pullers and owners by sending several written representations to the Hon'ble Chief Minister of the State and by personally meeting the Chief Minister in her office at Nabanna.

***Notes and References***


1. KPM/SB/0/036/05, File No. SW-994 of 1944, Government of West Bengal, Police Department, confidential, report by Sub-Inspector, B.K. Roy Chowdhury, dated 8.9.1944, Police Museum Archives, Kolkata.
2. Rules & Bye-laws of All Bengal Rickshaw Union, p.1
3. Rules & Bye-laws of all Bengal Rickshaw Union (ABRU), pp. 1-3.
4. Rules & Bye-laws of ABRU, pp. 4-5
5. Rules & Bye-laws of ABRU, pp. 5-6.
6. Rules & Bye-laws of ABRU, pp. 6-7.
7. Rules & Bye-laws of ABRU, p. 7.
8. Rules & Bye-laws of ABRU, p. 7.
9. Rules & Bye-laws of ABRU, p. 8.
10. Rules & Bye-laws of ABRU, pp. 9-10.
11. Rules & Bye-laws of ABRU, pp. 10-11.

12. Rules & Bye-laws of ABRU, pp. 11-12.
13. Rules & Bye-laws of ABRU, pp. 12-13.
14. Rules & Bye-laws of ABRU, pp. 14-16.
15. Rules & Bye-laws of ABRU, pp. 16-18.
16. Xerox copy of the Auditor's Report dated 23rd March, 1999, Kar, Sen & Co., Chartered Accountants, 19, British Indian Street, Calcutta – 700069.
17. List of Presidents and General Secretaries, 1960 to 2000, provided by Mukhtar Ali, General Secretary, ABRU.
18. Xerox copy of the Auditor's Report dated 7th March, 2001, Kar, Sen & Co., 19, British India Street, Calcutta – 700069.
19. Personal interview of Anwar Hussain taken by the author on 11.12.2022 at his rickshaw garage at Beniapukur Road, Kolkata.
20. Personal interview of Kishan Deo Yadav taken by the author on 12.12.2022 in his rickshaw garage at 219/A1, Picnic Garden Road, Kolkata – 700039.
21. KPM(SB)00851/05, File No.S.W. 822/1939, Government of West Bengal, Police Dept. Confidential, Kolkata Police Museum Archives.
22. KPM(SB) 00851/05, File No. S.W. 822/1939, Government of West Bengal, Police dept. Confidential, Kolkata Police Museum Archives.
23. KPM (SB) 00851/05, File No. S.W. 822/1939, Government of West Bengal, Police Dept. Confidential, Kolkata Police Museum Archives.
24. KPM (SB) 00851/05, File No. S.W. 822/1939, op. cit.
25. KPM (SB) 00851/05, File No. S.W. 822/1939, op. cit.
26. KPM (SB) 00851/05, File No. S.W. 822/1939, op. cit.
27. KPM/SB/0/036/05, file No. SW-994 of 1944, Report by B.K. Roy Chowdhury, Sub-Inspector, Calcutta Police, Special Branch, Report dated 07.08.1944, Kolkata Police Museum Archives.
28. KPM/SB/0/036/05, File No. SW-994 of 1944, Police

Department, Confidential, Kolkata Police Museum Archives.

29. KPM/SB/0/036/05, File No. SW-994 of 1944, op. cit & Report by B.K. Roy Choudhury dated 24.08.1944.
30. KPM/SB/0/036/05, File No. SW-944 of 1944, op. cit.
31. KPM/SB/0/036/05, File No. SW-944 of 1944, op.cit.
32. KPM/SB/0/036/05, File No. SW-944 of 1944, op.cit.
33. KPM/SB/0/036/05, File No. SW-944 of 1944, op.cit.
34. KPM/SB/0/036/05, File No. SW-994 of 1944, op.cit.
35. KPM/SB/0/036/05, File No. SW-994 of 1944, op. cit.
36. KPM/SB/0/036/05, File No. SW-994 of 1944, op. cit.
37. KPM/SB/0/036/05, File No. SW-994 of 1944, op. cit.
38. KPM/SB/0/036/05, File No. SW-994 of 1944, op.cit.
39. KPM/SB/0/036/05, File No. SW-994 of 1944, op. cit.
40. Thomas, Dr. T.H., 'Rickshaws in Caclutta', a report in association with Unnayan, AIIPH, Caclutta, February 1981, p. 26.
41. Thomas, Dr. T.H., 'Rickshaws in Calcutta', a report in association with Unnayan, AIIPH at 36/1A, Garcha Road, Calcutta-19, Calcutta, February, 1981, pp. 26-27.
42. Xerox copy of a letter dated 19th September, 1996 written on the letterhead of Noor Ahmed and Ganpati Jha of Calcutta Rickshaw Chalak Panchayat and addressed to Mr. Subhas Chakravarty, Minister of Transport & Sports, Government of West Bengal.
43. Xerox copy of a letter dated 25.09.1996 written by Abdul Wahab on the letterhead of ABRU and addressed to Sm. Mamata Banerjee.
44. The **Statesman** newspaper, dated 25.06.2011, Calcutta.
45. The **Statesman** newspaper, dated 26.06.2011, Kolkata.
46. The **Statesman** newspaper, dated 07.07.2011, Kolkata.
47. The **Statesman** newspaper, dated 07.07.2011, Kolkata.

# Chapter IV

## Present Rickshaw Owners and Pullers

The present owners of rickshaws, like their pullers are primarily outsiders and non-Bengali. Majority of them are hailing from different districts of Bihar and Jharkhand and a few are from U.P. Many of these owners have been pullers in the past. Many of them have not worked their way up from below and many combine ownership of rickshaws with that of slum property, called cattle sheds and other informal assets. Hand rickshaws are not owned by limited companies or co-operatives nor are they hypothecated to banks[1].

Most of the rickshaw owners and pullers are hindi speaking Biharis and a few of them are living in Calcutta with their families. These pullers are all male. Their origins, their families and their land are predominantly in Mazaffarpur, Samastipur and Monghyr districts of Bihar. They are attracted to Calcutta by the prospect of a monetary income sufficient to lift them out of their rural poverty and to enable them to withstand long standing domination by higher castes in Bihar. In consequence many of them minimise expenditure on themselves in order to remit most of their income to their families living in their native place.

The rickshaw owners and pullers are Hindus and Muslims by religion[2].

In order to save their income the rickshawpullers who live in Calcutta alone, have been living a community life viz living together in the rickshaw khatal or garage of their owner and sharing a common mess where they are cooking food and eating together. In such common mess the pullers' financial contribution is much less than what they would have to pay if they lived separately. Some of these pullers, 20 to 25 of them also rent a common kitchen and a room in a slum where they store their belongings. The pullers take turns in preparing meals for which a daily charge or levy is collected. The pullers hardly have any breakfast but they eat a meal of onion, green chilly and chhatu (powdered pulse) in the early afternoon and chapati (hand made wheat bread) and dal (pulse) at night. Though the puller's work is painstaking and tiresome, his diet is insufficient and meagre for good health. Many rickshawpullers whose owners do not have a rickshaw garage to stay overnight, their sleeping place is mostly the footpath or a verandah. A few pullers obtain living space by acting as night watchmen in factories or shops. Some pullers sleep with their vehicles parked on the road. Their dress is normally a dhoti and fatua (a loose T-shirt with buttons) or a T-shirt, shirt or vest for hindu pullers and a lungi and vest or T-shirt for muslim pullers[3].

As regards the location of the rickshaw pullers, they are found waiting for passengers on the lanes and bye-lanes all over Calcutta in north Calcutta, central Calcutta and south Calcutta except the main roads where they are prohibited by the police from entering. Sometimes rickshaw pullers are seen plying on the main roads with passengers or goods violating traffic rules, entering the Gariahat Road, Rashbehari Avenue, Southern Avenue, Lake Road, Harish Mukherjee Road, Jadu Babur Bazar's Road in the south, Central Avenue, Shyambazar, Shobhabazar and Bagbazar main roads in the north. The pullers are also found carrying passengers and goods on their vehicles in Sealdah, Burrabazar and Khiderpore areas[4].

Social life of the pullers is very limited due to lack of both money and family. The muslim and the hindu pullers observe their religious festivals. Smoking is common among them – ganja (cannabis) for the older men and bidi and khainei (cheap tobacco leaves) for the young men. A puller, who owns land in his native place, usually visits his village for a month or more once a year to meet his family members and to attend to either sowing or harvesting. Muslim pullers who are generally landless spend shorter time in their villages[5].

Rickshawpulling is a socially acceptable activity. But in Calcutta society however a rickshawpuller has a low status[5a].

Between 10% and 30% of the pullers have their families with them in Calcutta. But since their average income is not sufficient, their life style is poor and most of them are found living with their families in the slums in and around Calcutta[6].

Very few rickshaw pullers own their own vehicles, less than one in a hundred do. The normal custom in this trade is for a puller to rent his vehicle from a fleet owner on a shift basis. The owner takes responsibility for the costs keeping the vehicle in service including payment for repair, licensing and any overnight garaging. The puller collects and returns the rickshaw for each hire period and undertakes routine maintenance and cleaning. If a puller's annual income is around Rs.3,500/-, one-third of this will go to pay for his own subsistence in Calcutta and the rest will be posted home to support his dependants[7].

The puller of an unlicensed vehicle often has other costs such as loss of earnings when his vehicle is impounded or a bribe of a rupee a day to prevent that happening. In fact even pullers of licensed vehicles also have to pay regularly some sort of small payments for immunity from harassment by local police. Rickshaws are usually taken out in two shifts – morning and evening shifts. However night service is available in case of emergency. The rickshaw fare varies from area to area and there is no uniform fixed rate based on the distance of the road to which the puller will take the passenger. Presently the puller charges higher rate of fare, sometimes exorbitant rate, compared to previous moderate rates which the puller used to charge from the passengers[8].

From the owner's point of view a licensed rickshaw is a lucrative investment, offering a return on capital of between 100 to 150% per annum, depending on the fleet's size. The average fleet size may be 5 rickshaws. There is no provision for depreciation since the allowance for repairs is sufficient for replacement of worn parts. Overnight garaging costs are often avoided by keeping the rickshaws on the pavement[9].

***Ramrit Paswan*** was the oldest rickshawpuller in Calcutta. He lived in a bustee (slum) in central Calcutta. He is known in that area as 'Burra Baba'. In 1920 at the age of 23 he landed in Calcutta from Samastipur in Bihar and sought employment in the rickshaw trade. He retired at the age of 60 in 1980. He recollected that in those days rickshaws operated from a few stands – Bentinck Street, Hogg Market, the Grand Hotel, Medical College and the two railway stations at Sealdah and Howrah. The office goers and court goers at that time used rickshaws. There was no restriction on movement of rickshaws in those days nor police harassment. Ramrit lived in Das Lane (in the area opposite the present Indian Airlines Office on Chittaranjan Avenue), a rickshaw puller's centre. He earned 8 to 10 annas a day and also getting 3 annas extra baksheesh (tips) for a trip of a mile or two[10].

It is interesting to note in this connection that in the 1930s two educated young Bengalis of the bhadralok (gentleman) class took rickshaw pulling as an occupation. Their spirit of self-help and moral courage were praisewarthy[11].

The rickshaw trade is labour intensive which includes not only rickshaw owners and pullers but also sardars or agents and rickshaw repairing craftsmen. Many rickshaw owners at present appoint one of his rickshaw pullers or any other puller a sardar whose duty is to supervise this business and he is paid according to the size of the owner's fleet. The sardar's duty is to renew the puller's licence and owner's licence, to arrange for the repair of the rickshaw and to look after the police cases in connection with rickshaws. The owner of the rickshaw does not pay any monthly salary to a sardar but only a percentage from the day's earning of a rickshaw. Hand pulled rickshaws are made wholly and repaired by rickshaw repairing craftsmen who have been formally trained in this work by their predecessors viz grandfather, father or any other relative skilled in this work for many years. In the rickshaw garages existing still today, the author has found rickshaw repairing craftsmen who are busy with the work of repairing the old rickshaws. Thus these two categories of people, viz. the sardars and the rickshaw repairing craftsmen also form an integral part of the rickshaw trade[12].

**Interactions with the present hand pulled rickshaw owners and pullers :**

The author met some rickshaw pullers waiting for passengers in the rickshaw stand near the entrance gate of the ***Gariahat Market*** in south Calcutta. One of them, ***Bablu Haldar***, aged 50 years, has been pulling rickshaw for the last 22 years. He lives with his family at 1, Mukundapur Road. He is a Bengali Hindu. ***Sunil Sardar***, another puller, aged about 55 years has been pulling rickshaw for over 30 years and Dhurup Shaw is his rickshaw owner having around 80 rickshaws. Sunil lives with his wife and two children in a colony at Bosepukur, Kolkata 700042. Sunil informed the author that he has to pay the owner of the rickshaw Rs.40/- per day. ***Sona Mondal***, aged 45 years, has been pulling rickshaw for around 25 years only in two shifts viz. morning and afternoon and he earns around Rs.250 to 300/- per day. He is married and stays with his family at Dhakuria. Both Sunil and Sona are also Bengali Hindu[13].

Near the handpulled rickshaw stand outside the *New Market* (formerly Hogg Market) on the *Linsay Street*, Kolkata, the author found a few pullers. One of them, was ***Jamiruddin Jamal***, aged 52 years. He hails from Barharwa village under Motihar district in Bihar. He has been pulling rickshaw from 9-00 a.m. to 5-00 p.m. for 10/12 years and earns Rs.200/- to 300/- per day. His rickshaw's owner is Aitul who has got 6 rickshaws and who stays at Taltala. Jamiruddin has to pay Rs.30/- every day to the owner. His wife and four children live in his native place His owner's rickshaw garage is located at Mehendi Bagan, Taltola. He informed the author that he has to pay a fine of Rs.80/- to the traffic police 2/3 times every month, even in case the police catches him standing with the rickshaw at the stand. ***Sk. Nazim***, another puller, aged 30 years hails from Laukhan village in Motihari district in Bihar. He has been pulling rickshaw for 15/16 years. Both Jamiruddin and Sk. Nazim have got no landed property at home. Nazim came to Calcutta for the first time with a villager from his village who also is a hand rickshaw puller. Nazim pulls rickshaw in the Burrabazar Street, Zakaria Street and near Sealdah Station. He earns Rs.250/- to 300/- per day and has to pay Rs.50/- to his owner everyday as he pulls rickshaw from 7-00 a.m. to 8-00 p.m. He sends around Rs.5,000/- to Rs.7,000/- to his family every month. ***Mohammad Tohid***, aged 45 years, hails from Daryapur village under district Samastipur in Bihar. He has been pulling rickshaw for 17/18 years. Like Nazim, Tohid also came to Calcutta for the first time, along with another puller from his village. He pulls rickshaw from 7-00 a.m. to 8-00 p.m. and pays Rs.30/- per day to the owner. His rickshaw owner is Aitul, who has a rickshaw garage at 29, Alimuddin Street. Md. Tohid earns Rs.350/- to Rs.400/- per day. He has to pay Rs.80/- to the traffic police twice a month. Tohid further informed the author that the policemen of Muchipara Police Station charge Rs.100/- from him if they catch him at the stand. He takes food in a cheap hotel and pays from his pocket. All these three rickshaw pullers in the New Market area are Bihari muslims and they do not stay and eat in a common mess[14].

At ***10, Cornfield Road***, in south Calcutta, the

author met a few handrickshaw pullers who were waiting for passengers at the rickshaw stand. One of them, ***Nandu Shaw***, aged 52 years and hailing from Delawarpur under district Motihari in Bihar, has been pulling rickshaw for the last 16/17 years. He stated that he came to Calcutta along with a villager of his village who was also a handrickshawpuller. He pulls rickshaw from 7-00 a.m. to 8-00 p.m. and earns Rs.200/- to Rs.300/- per day. On days when schools are open his daily income is more i.e. Rs.400/- to Rs.500/-. Nandu Shaw informed the author that there is no garage for keeping his rickshaw and so he keeps his rickshaw on the footpath and fellow pullers and himself have a rented room (dera) in a slum at 1, Kankulia Road. Another puller, ***Misrilal Yadav***, aged 46 years, and hailing from Subaiya village under Matihari district in Bihar, has been pulling rickshaw for the last 20 years. He earns around Rs.500/- per day and he has to pay Rs.30/- per day to the owner of the rickshaw. His family lives in his native place. He has 3 bighas of agricultural land which he cultivates with the help of labourers. ***Sudhan Das***, aged 50 years, hailing from Subaiya village, district Motihari in Bihar, has been pulling rickshaw for 15 years. He first came to Calcutta along with a villager of his village. He earns Rs.300/- to Rs.400/- per day and pays Rs.20/- to his owner per week. His owner, Bishaldeo Roy has a rickshaw garage in Picnic Garden Road where there are around 100 rickshaws. Rickshaws are repaired in this garage. These rickshaws are pulled in different routes like Jogubaburbazar, Bhawanipur, Golpark, Lake Market, Burrabazar and so on. If the State Government forbids pulling of hand rickshaw on the streets of Calcutta, he is willing to drive a three wheeler ('Toto') if Toto is provided by the government. ***Budar Das***, aged 61 years, also hailing from village Sumaiya of Motihari district in Bihar has been pulling a rickshaw for the last 22 years and he earns Rs.200/- to Rs.500/- per day[15].

***Prakash Shaw***, aged around 33 years, has a rickshaw khatal/garage at 7, Nebubagan Lane, Kolkata – 700003. His house is inside this garage. Prakash tells us that he hails from Varanasi in U.P. and the last four generations of his family had been in rickshaw business as owners. His father, ***Shiv Saran Shaw***, aged 63 years is still the owner of this Khatal. They have got 14 rickshaws which ply in Shyambazar and Bagbazar areas in north Calcutta. Prakash Shaw informs us that every month his father has to pay Rs.150/- to the local Shyampukur Police Station and Rs.150/- to the local traffic guard who visits their house and collect the money. Every rickshawpuller has to pay Rs.150/- per week to him while in the Burrabazar area a rickshaw puller has to pay more, viz. Rs.200/- per week to the owner. Since 2007/2008 licence renewal of the hand pulled rickshaws had been stopped. Prakash Shaw finally tells us that all the pullers of their rickshaws stay in their garage and they eat in a common mess. A few rickshawpullers have now become drivers of private taxis, OLA and UBER after learning driving of four wheelers vehicles[16].

***Mahesh Yadav***, aged 45 years, hailing from Gurua village under district Gaya in Bihar, has been pulling rickshaw for the last 5/6 years and his rickshaw owner is Prakash Shaw. He earns around Rs.400/- per day and he pays Rs.25/- per day to the owner. He first came to Calcutta along with another rickshaw puller of his village. He has got 15 Kathas of land and during monsoon he visits his native place for the purpose of cultivating his land. He keeps the rickshaw in the owner's Khatal and has his meal there in common mess by contributing his share of money. Finally he tells us that if rickshaw is banned totally, he is willing to drive a 'toto' if he gets one.

***Sudeswar Yadav***, aged 55 years, hailing from village Maliachawk in Gaya district in Bihar has been pulling rickshaw for the last 25 years. He earns around Rs.300/- per day, sends Rs.100/- to his family in Bihar and pays Rs.30/- per day to the owner of the rickshaw. He keeps the rickshaw in the rickshaw garage at Nebubagan and sleeps on the footpath. His father, Babulal used to pull rickshaw on this route and thereafter he came to Calcutta with his father and started pulling rickshaw. Many of his relatives also pull rickshaw here. If rickshaw is banned by the government, he will look for an alternative job or else go back home[17].

***Hari Charan Yadav***, aged 56 years, hailing from Baragaon village in Uttar Pradesh, has been pulling rickshaw since 1990. He pulls rickshaw since 7-00 a.m. till night. His rickshaw owner is Rahman Mia who also hails from U.P. and whose rickshaw garage is in Beniapukur. Haricharan earns Rs.300/- per day. He has got 20 kathas of land in which he cultivates paddy, wheat and vegetables during summer. He has to pay Rs.30/- to the owner every day while the owner pays for the repairing cost of the rickshaw as well as pays Rs.100/- as fine to the police. His owner has 10 rickshaws which ply in Shyambazar & Bagbazar area upto to Sealdah[18].

***Mukhtar Ali***, at present the ***General Secretary*** of ***All Bengal Rickshaw Union***, informs the author that his family was involved in the rickshaw business for a long time. His father, though working outside Calcutta, purchased one rickshaw in his name, one rickshaw in his mother's name and a few rickshaws in his father's name. In 1998 Mukhtar Ali, after passing Higher Secondary Examination, became the acting General Secretary of the All Bengal Rickshaw Union (ABRU). At that time Kalimuddin Sams was the President and Somnath Chatterjee and Sanat Kumar Banerjee were joint Vice-Presidents of ABRU. Thereafter Soumen Mitra and subsequently Sultan Ahmed were the Presidents of ABRU. At present Kashinath Paul has been the President since 2016. Mukhtar Ali further states that the office of the Rickshaw Union at 51, Chittaranjan Avenue is now almost closed and the people connected with the rickshaw business have lost all hope and expectations due to the indifferent attitude of the State Government. Mr. Ali, finally tells us that he has been paying the rent of the Union's office for the last 10 years from his own pocket since no income of the Union is coming forth. For the last 12 years or so he has been looking after the case for eviction of Union filed by the landlord and rent is being deposited in the Rent Control Office. According to him many handrickshaw pullers have subsequently become owners and now more owners of rickshaws are muslims[19].

***Anwar Hussain***, a rickshaw owner cum sardar, aged around 62 years, hails from village Ganiyari, district Mujaffarpur in Bihar. He came to Calcutta in 1965 and his father Late Hussain Bux was a rickshaw owner. After his father's death, his elder brother, Moh. Muslim looked after this business and after his brother's death Anwar Hussain has been looking after this business since 1991. His residence at Beniapukur Road is partly a rickshaw khatal. This khatal and residence is rented and it belongs to a wakf. Anwar's father had 40 rickshaws. During 1980 to 1991 his elder brother had 10 rickshaws of his own while 70 rickshaws belonging to others were garaged here. During his father's time every rickshaw puller had to pay Re.1.25 paise per day and repairing work of rickshaw was done in this garage at that time for which separate charges were paid. In 1980 to 1991 every rickshaw had to pay Rs.6/- per day as rent. From 1991 till 2006 there were 85 rickshaws in this garage, out of which 22 were owned by Anwar. At present this business is almost closed and now only two of his rickshaws are plying on the road. In his garage the rickshaw pullers live in common mess and prepare food by forming separate groups (hindu rickshaw pullers and muslim rickshawpullers). Anwar informs us that rickshaw licences are 3 in number viz. Police licence (Rs.10/-), Corporation licence (Rs.15/-) and Trade licence or owner's licence (Rs.15/-) per year. The rickshaw puller's licence was not issued or renewed since 1980. The rickshaws have to pay around Rs.200/- as fines per month to the Police for keeping the rickshaw on 'no parking' zone. For the purpose of C.F. the owner has to get the rickshaw repaired and coloured which cost around Rs.4,000/- while the maintenance cost of a rickshaw is around Rs.10,000/-. Now the rickshaw repairmen are not so easily available as they mostly come from Bihar. Anwar Hussain has been a member of ABRU by paying a fee of Rs.10/- annually. He paid this fee upto 2007. He further informs us that there are around 1000 women rickshaw owners who are all wives of male rickshaw owners. But they do not play any active role in the rickshaw business. 20% of these women rickshaw owners are hindus while the rest owners are muslim women owners[20].

***Kishan Deo Yadav***, aged 50 years, hailing from village Parasiya under district Buxar in Bihar, is an owner of hand pulled rickshaws and has a rickshaw garage at 219/A1, Picnic Garden Road, Kolkata - 700039. He resides at 211/D, Picnic Garden Road, Kolkata - 700039. He tells as that he came to Calcutta in 1980 at the age of 10 years. His father, Mahamgu Yadav was a Police Constable in the Calcutta Police. This garage originally belonged to his paternal uncle's two sons, viz. Anbhu Yadav and Bishnudeo Yadav. Kishan Deo Yadav further informs us that after passing Higher Secondary Examination, he joined this business as an apprentice under Anbhu Yadav. For over two years he worked as a rickshaw puller in the route starting from Bondel Gate to Gariahat and upto Ballygunge Phari. He pulled rickshaw till the end of 2004. Since 1992 upto 20 years he was a joint partner in this business. Thereafter he started buying rickshaws at the rate of Rs.12,000/- to Rs.13,000/-. He had 100 rickshaws of his own in 2015. His rickshaws ply in Bondel Gate area, Hazra Crossing, Ballygunge Station Road, Cornfield Road, Gariahat Market, Golpark area below Dhakuria Bridge. He also worked as a sardar and hired pullers for pulling his rickshaws. In 2000 he had 30 rickshaws and at that time till the ban was imposed on rickshaws trade in 2007, he had a thriving rickshaw business and his monthly income was Rs.20,000/- or more. As a sardar he used to earn Rs.200/- per rickshaw per month and the owner used to get Rs.400/- per rickshaw per month. At present himself and his uncle's brother have got 150 rickshaws of which he has 80/90 rickshaws of his own. The rickshaw puller pays Rs.30/- per day to him. He also states that the trade licence,

Corporation licence and Police licence were renewed in the year 2006 for the last time. Now his rickshaws are operating without any valid licence, since the government has stopped issuing new licence[21].

Kishan Deo asserts that after the Government has banned the hand pulled rickshaw in Calcutta, many rickshaw pullers have left this city and have gone back home. Now Kishan Deo has 40 rickshaws of his own and now his rickshaws are plying in Bhabanipur area near Jadu Babur Bazar (10 rickshaws), in Lake Market area (6 rickshaws), in Gariahat Market near its main gate, (10 rickshaws), in Ballygunge Station Stand (6 rickshaws), in Cornfield Road, Bondel Gate and Ballygunge Place. He also acts as a sardar for others rickshaws. At present he earns Rs.30,000/- to Rs.35,000/- per month as net income after deducting all expenditure. Each of his pullers pay him a fee of Rs.30/- per day. Kishan Deo has been a member of All Bengal Rickshaw Union for the last 25 to 30 years and he used to pay Rs.10/- to the Union as annual subscription. He has been a member of the Executive Committee of the Union. Prior to 2006 he used to earn around Rs.40,000/- per month in rickshaw business. But now he is earning 25% less than what he earned before. All his rickshaws are now kept on the footpath as there is no garage. The rickshawpullers working under him, live together in 4/5 rooms rented in a slum at 1, Kankulia Road, Kolkata – 700019 and they cook and eat in a joint mess[22].

Kishan Deo further informs us that the garage at 219/A1, Picnic Garden Road is for the purpose of repairing old rickshaws and constructing new rickshaws. All garages for repair have closed down since 2006. Now only two garages viz. this garage and Dhurup Shaw's garage at 40P, Dr. G.S. Bose Road, Kolkata – 700039 are operating in south Calcutta. In this two garages now only Kishan Deo's and Dhurup Shaw's rickshaws are repaired and new rickshaws are made also. Previously other owner's rickshaws were repaired in this two garages. They pay the rickshaw craftsmen Rs.250/- to Rs.300/- per day for doing repairing work[23].

Kishan Deo tells us that a hand pulled rickshaw has to have two kinds of licences – Police licence to be renewed annually and trade licence of the amount of Rs.10/- to be renewed yearly. The trade licence fee as increased from Rs.30/- to / Rs.35/- for the last time. Previously the Police officer at 16, Canal Road used to issue the Police licence in two copies – one copy for the owner and the other copy for the puller. But now this office has shifted to Hackney Carriage Department's office near Princep Ghat. The Corporation licence was issued from its office at 5, S.N. Banerjee Raod in the main building's office on the ground floor. S. Thakur was the last issuing officer in the Kolkata Municipal Corporation[24].

Finally Kishan Deo opines that if the Government allows e-rickshaws to ply on the roads, it will help in the rehabilitation of rickshaw pullers and the owners and it will save the rickshaw business from being closed down. He has three sons and one daughter – eldest son, Manish Yadav, is a Chef working in a hotel in France after completing Hotel Management Course from the International Institute of Hotel Management at Sector-V, Salt Lake City, second son, Brijesh Yadav, is a MBBS student in Calcutta Medical College after qualifying in NET Examination. He got admission in the OBC quota, his youngest son is reading in Class-XII while his daughter Neha Yadav is an undergraduate student doing B.Com. in Deshbandhu Womens' College. She is now preparing for appearing in UPSC Examination. None of his children likes the rickshaw trade nor has any wish to join this business. Kishen Deo finally states that Mr. Mukhtar Ali, General Secretary of All Bengal Rickshaw Union helped him a lot in obtaining the OBC certificate for his second son and in getting admission to the College for his daughter[25].

***Tenny Sharma***, a rickshaw craftsman, tells us that he has been working in the garage at 219/A1, Picnic Garden Road, Kolkata – 700039, for many years. He came to Calcutta from Bihar at the age of 12 years and he learnt the repairing work from his father, Late Sohan Thakur Sharma. It takes around 3 to 4 hours to repair one wheel of a hand pulled rickshaw. It takes 12 to 13 hours to make a new wheel. He further states himself along with Parameswar Sharma, another craftsman also do the body repairing of a rickshaw viz. changing the seat mattress, seat cover and the hood of the rickshaw. Keshan Deo pays him Rs.250/- to Rs.300/- per day[26].

***Parameswar Sharma***, now aged 70 years, came to Calcutta from village Rusulpur under Vaisali district in Bihar. He has been working as a rickshaw craftsman in the aforesaid garage for the last 10 years[27].

***Dhurup Lal Shaw***, aged 60 years, hailing from village Dautpur in Chapra district of Bihar, first came to Calcutta at the tender age of 12 years along with his father, Late Nageswar Lal Shaw. His father was a Sadar and started a rickshaw garage at 40P, Dr. G.S. Bose Road, Kolkata – 700039 (near Sahebbagan). Both repair work and construction of new rickshaws are done in this garage. Around 1970 Dhurup Shaw joined his father's business. At that time his father had 10 rickshaws of his own while his father took other owners' rickshaws on the basis of commission like Rs.20/- per day. Subsequently Dhurup Shaw took over this business in 1980 and for the last 40 years he is the sole owner of this business. Now he has got 28 rickshaws and his rickshaws ply in Ballygunge area, Lake Road, Bhawanipur, Kalighat and Bondel Road[28].

Dhurup Shaw informs us that when he first joined this business with his father, the puller used to pay the owner Rs.2/- per day. In 1986 this rate was increased to Rs.7/- per day, in 1990-95 the rate was further increased to Rs.10/- to Rs.15/- and in 1996 it was increased to Rs.20/- per day. Since 1996 till date this rate was increased to Rs.30/- per day. The last new licence for the hand pulled rickshaw was issued by the Government in 2006. In his opinion the new generation of the present rickshaw owners will not join this business as because their children are now getting educated and after completion of their studies, they will take up jobs as per their academic qualifications[29].

***Ramdhani Sharma***, aged 69 years and hailing from village Sidhauli in Vaisali district in Bihar, came to Calcutta in 1965 with his father, Late Daroga Sharma, at the age of 11/12 years. His father had a shop dealing in iron goods at Bowbazar. In 1980 Ramdhani started a business of supplying building materials. In the same year he also bought 16 handrickshaws at the price of Rs.10,500/- per rickshaw and joined the rickshaw business. He also took possession of the rickshaw garage at 236, B.B. Ganguly Street on the basis of a contract in 1978 with N.R. Patel, a Gujarati gentleman. He started paying him Rs.500/- as monthly rent. For the last

15/20 years he has been paying his landlord Rs.5,000/- per month as rent[30].

Ramdhani states that though he has 50 rickshaws, now only 20/25 rickshaws are being pulled on the road as during amphan cyclone and covid epidemic, many of his rickshaws were damaged beyond repair. Now he has 20 rickshaws in his name, 16 rickshaws in the name of Manoj, his eldest son, 10 rickshaws in the name of Rajkumar, his youngest son, 5 rickshaws in the name of his wife, Dharamseela Devi and 10 rickshaws in the name of Hiralal Sharma, his paternal uncle's son. His eldest son is a manager in the Computer Engineering College at Salt Lake City, Sector-5, while his other son works in a call centre and they do not like this rickshaw business. His rickshaws ply on the roads of north Calcutta like B.B. Ganguly Street, Ganesh Chandra Avenue, Nirmal Chandra Street, Muktarambabu Street, CIT Road, Kalabagan, the locality near the Medical College, Jorabagan, Malapara, Ganesh Talkies, Girish Park, Singibagan, Sealdah N.R.S. Hospital and so on. Ramdhani informs us that the owner of the rickshaw has to pay all fines and cost of repair of the rickshaw. He has to pay Rs.200/- per month to the police constables of Bowbazar Police Station, dealing with petty cases and he pays Rs.500/- per month to the Traffic Police. In case a rickshaw is caught in a petty case, he has to pay Rs.100/- to the Police[31].

Ramdhani Sharma states further that previously the rickshaw pullers who worked under him used to stay in the rooms in his rickshaw garage. During 1980s and 1990s many rickshaw pullers used to stay in his garage and they had food in a common mess by cooking food together and contributing their share of money. Now only a few pullers stay in this garage as many pullers are now living with their families in separate accommodation[32].

Since the year 1985/86 Ramdhani Sharma had been an ordinary member of All Bengal Rickshaw Union. In 1990 he became a member of the Executive Committee of the Union. The membership fee is Rs.10/- annually for ordinary member and Rs.20/- annually for a member of Executive Committee. There were 36 members in this Committee till 2006. Now there are 32 members as 4 of them had passed away. Ramdhani states that prior to 1980 a doctor used to sit in the Union's Office. There was a darwan, a cashier and 4 persons who looked after the police cases. This 4 persons were paid staff of the Union. He states that the Hackney Carriage department used to issue owners' licence or police licence which was called trade licence while pullers' licence was issued in two copies, one for the puller and one for the owner. The number written on the back of every rickshaw was originally given by the Hackney Carriage Department under the British Government[33].

Ramdhani Sharma is an ex-member of the *Rickshaw Workers' Union* at 249, B.B. Ganguly Street. The office of this Union has been closed in 1993 after the death of Mayaram Roy (13.1.93) who was its Secretary. Durganath Ghosh was the Vice-President of this Union. Ramdhani used to pay Rs.25/- as membership fee annually. He joined this Union in 1985/86. This Union used to look after the renewal of pullers' licence and dealt with the pullers' petty case in the local police stations[34].

Finally Ramdhani informs us that 80% of the rickshaw owners are muslims and 20% of them are hindus who came mostly from Bihar and U.P.

Before 1990s many hindus and muslims from 24 Parganas, (north & south) came to him for rickshaw pulling work. But from 1990s till date more muslims from 24-Parganas (South) have been coming to him for seeking work of rickshaw pulling. In his rickshaw garage 80% of his rickshaws are garaged at night and his rickshaws are only repaired in his garage by the rickshaw craftsmen. Ramdhani Sharma is a sardar in respect of the rickshaws in the name of his wife, his sons, his brother's son, his elder brother and his brother's wife. During the period from 1980-1990 he was a sardar in respect of 175 rickshaws. The muslim owners mostly appoint sardars to look after their rickshaws[35].

Ramdhani Sharma along with other owners and pullers agitated for 8 hours and made a dharna near Gandhiji's statue in 2015/16 demanding rehabilitation of the pullers and owners[36].

The author interviewed *two rickshaw pullers* working under Ramdhani Sharma. One of them, ***Moh. Israil***, aged 50 years and hailing from village Jambu Jamdar in district Giridih in Jharkhand, has been pulling rickshaw for a long time. He first came to Calcutta with his brother-in-law who worked in CESC. His family stays in his native place. He has got 10 kathas of agricultural land. He goes home in the monsoon season to cultivate his land and he grows paddy, potato, barley etc. He earns Rs.250/- to Rs.300/- per day and he pays Rs.20/- to his Sardar per day. His trade licence has not been renewed after 1980. If Government bans rickshaw pulling he will go back home. ***Moh. Salem***, aged 62 years came to Calcutta from village Barpukur Samela in district Darbhanga in Bihar. He came to Calcutta at the age of 12 years as an orphan and started pulling rickshaw. Since 2018 till date he has been pulling rickshaw under Ramdhani Sharma. He earns Rs.200/- to Rs.250/- per day and he has to pay Rs.15/- to Rs.20/- to the Sardar per day. If rickshaw pulling is banned by the Government, he will have to beg for survival[37].

The author also interviewed *two rickshaw repairmen or craftsmen* in the garage at 236, B.B. Ganguly Street, Kolkata. ***Ram Ekbal Sharma***, aged 65 years, hailing from village Paygamparpur in district Muzaffarpur in Bihar, came to Calcutta 50 years ago at the age of 10/11 years, with his paternal aunt's husband who was a rickshaw repairman. His aunt's husband used to stay in a rickshaw garage at Priyonath Mullick Road in Bhawanipur. He learnt the work of rickshaw repairing from his aunt's husband. At first he started work in the aforesaid garage and worked for 8 years. Thereafter he worked in a garage of Babunand Singh located behind Ramrick Hospital, as well as in the garage of Haribabu at Chakraberia Road. Subsequently he joined the garage of Ramdhani Sharma at 236, B.B. Ganguly Street, Kolkata – 700012 in October, 2022. He is getting Rs.400/- per day for his rickshaw repairing work. His family stays at home in his native place. If rickshaw pulling is banned he will have to go back home as there is no other option. ***Chandreswar Sharma***, aged 65 years, came to Calcutta from village Rusulpur Gangti, in district Vaishali in Bihar in 1970 with his elder brother who was involved in this rickshaw repairing work. His brother used to work in a rickshaw garage at 10, Kankulia Road and he worked there for 15 years. Thereafter he joined a garage at Keshab Chandra Sen Street at Rajabazar and had worked there for 40 years. He gets Rs.400/- per day from the owner of the garage. If rickshaw business is banned by the Government he will have no other option but to go back home[38].

***Kashinath Paul*** aged 78 years, is the *President of the All Bengal Rickshaw Union* at present. Since 1980 he has been involved in the hand pulled rickshaw business. He started this business by buying two rickshaws only. He bought the rickshaws at the rate of Rs.6,000/- to Rs.7,000/- for one. Within 3/4 years he gradually increased the number of his rickshaws to 15. His rickshaws ply in College Street, Sealdah, Bowbazar upto the Sealdah Station. He has handed over his rickshaws to a Sardar viz Jagadish Jadav living in Potuatala Lane. Upto the year 2006, his 15 rickshaws were in full operation. But now only 6 to 8 of his rickshaws are running on the road. Kashinath Paul further informs us that previously he used to get Rs.16/- to Rs.17/- per day per rickshaw from the Sardar while the Sardar used to collect Rs.22/- to Rs.25/- per day from the puller. He became a member of ABRU by paying an annual fee of Rs.10/- after he bought two rickshaws. Subsequently he became a member of the Executive Committee of the Union after 1980. In 1984-85 he became the Cashier of the Union and in 2008-09 he became the President of the Union. Now there are 35 members in that Executive Committee of the Union. He opines that e-rickshaws should be allowed by the Government for rehabilitation of rickshaw pullers[39].

***Swapan Kumar Roy***, aged 81 years is a *rickshaw owner*. He informs us that his father, Late Siddheswar Roy was a rickshaw owner and bought a rickshaw in 1953 in his son's name. At that time Swapan Kumar Roy was a school student of Class-VI. Later on his father bought more rickshaws, around 21 rickshaws – some in his mother's name and some in Swapan Kumar's name. Subsequently after his mother's death in 1973, Swapan Kumar became the owner of all 21 rickshaws. These rickshaws run in Jorasanko, Burrabazar, Jorabangan, Battala and Shyampukur area. He asserts that since his father's time they had a rickshaw garage at 21/2A, Mahendra Goswami Lane, Kolkata – 700006 which is still in existence and all his rickshaws are parked in this garage. Since the year 2021 the repairing work of rickshaws had been closed in this garage as he no longer can afford the cost of employing rickshaw repairmen. At present he has 13 rickshaws plying on the road. He has delegated the responsibility of his rickshaws to a Sadar, Tarakanta Yadav who had gone home. So now a puller, Munia Razzak is working as a Sardar for his rickshaws. Swapan Kumar Roy states that many pullers are cultivators and they do not pull rickshaw throughout the year but only during the time when cultivation is over. So now there is dirth of pullers[40].

Swapan Kumar Roy became an ordinary member of ABRU in 1953 by paying an annual fee of Rs.5/- to Rs.6/-. In the 1970s this fee was increased to Rs.10/-. In 1978 he became a member of the Executive Committee of the Union. At that time a doctor sat regularly in the Union office for the purpose of issuing fitness certificate to the rickshaw puller for the purpose of getting a puller's licence. This doctor was paid a monthly salary and he sat in the Union office till the year, 2000. Swapan Kumar Roy became the General Secretary of the Union in 2006-07. The principle activities of ABRU were to look after the welfare of the pullers and to deal with the police cases like petty cases, renewal of licence and so on. In case of emergency, the Union used to provide ration to the pullers. He further informs us that in the past rickshaw business was profitable for both the owner and the puller. In the 1950s he used to get 6 annas per day from a puller, in 1957 he got 50 paise per day from the puller while now he is getting Rs.150/- to Rs.200/- from the puller per week for one rickshaw[41].

Finally Swapan Kumar Roy tells us that on 15th December, 2014 himself along with 7/8 other members of ABRU went to Nabanna, met the Chief Minister and submitted a written representation praying for rehabilitation of the rickshaw pullers and owners. The Hon'ble Chief Minister assured them about the starting of e-rickshaws[42].

***Tulsi Shaw***, aged 40 years and hailing from Village Madrapur in district Nawada, in Bihar, is a rickshaw puller under Swapan Kumar Roy. He came to Calcutta with Abhar Yadav, his village neighbour who also pulls a rickshaw. He pulls a rickshaw from 8-00 a.m. to 6-00 p.m. in Burrabazar, Shyambazar, Girish Park and Manicktala areas. He earns Rs.200/- to 250/- per day and he pays Rs.30/- to his rickshaw owner. He stays on the footpath at 12, Beadon Street. His family is in his native place. His eldest son works in Mumbai. If e-rickshaw is permitted he will drive the same[43].

***Sanjay Yadav***, a puller, aged 35 years and hailing from village Bagdumba, district Bakor in Bihar, has been pulling rickshaw in Calcutta for many years. His father Gadal Yadav also used to pull a rickshaw. Sanjay came to Calcutta at the age of 12 with his father and he has been pulling the rickshaw of Sunil Mahato, the owner. He earns Rs.300/- to 400/- per day and has to pay Rs.30/- per day and Rs.1200/- per week to the owner of the rickshaw. His owner's rickshaw garage is located at 6, Ramdulal Sarkar Street, Kolkata – 700006. His owner has 25/26 rickshaws and all the rickshaws are parked in this garage at night. There is one rickshaw repairman working in this garage. Sanjay tells us that he sleeps on the footpath near this garage and has his meal in a local hotel. He is able to send around Rs.4,000/- to Rs.5,000/- to his wife and children at home. He has two sons and one daughter who are all school going and he visits his family occasionally. He stays at home for 3 to 4 months. His owner takes care of the rickshaws and pays for the cost of repair and also pays the fine of Rs.100/- to the local police in case of a police case. Finally Sanjay states that he is happy with his work of rickshaw pulling, but if hand rickshaw is banned, he will find an alternative job or if e-rickshaw is introduced, he will drive e-rickshaw for a living[44].

***Rajkumar Ghosh***, aged around 60 years is a rickshaw owner and resides at 28A, Nanda Mullick Lane, Kolkata – 700006. In his family he is the first to join this rickshaw business. His father, late Lakshmi Narayan Ghosh was a taxi driver who drove his own taxi. Rajkumar Ghosh for the first time, bought one hand pulled rickshaw at Rs.6,000/- in his younger brother's name in 1986. At that time he used to do rickshaw business at South Dum Dum, Nager Bazar with 8 to 10 rickshaws. Till 2006 he had 15 rickshaws – 5 in his brother's name, 7 in his wife's name and 3 rickshaws in his name. In 1989-1990 he took charge of 15 rickshaws as a Sardar by means of a written contract. In this contract business he paid for the maintenance of the rickshaws, fee for licence renewal as well as fine to the police in petty cases. He also had to pay Rs.100/- per month per rickshaw to the owner of these rickshaws. In 2000 he used to get Rs.120/- per week per rickshaw, in 2002-03 this amount increased to Rs.140/- per week per rickshaw and in 2006 this amount increased to Rs.150/- per week per rickshaw. Now he is getting Rs.150/- to Rs.200/- per week per rickshaw. Now many of the old rickshaw pullers have left Calcutta without informing him. It is very difficult to get new pullers which in turn causes financial loss to the owners. When the pullers who leave for home, come back to Calcutta, they join work with some other owner out of fear that they have to pay for the days they did not pull his rickshaws. Rajkumar Ghosh joined ABRU in 2000 as an ordinary member and subsequently he became a member of the Executive Committee of the Union around 2004. His rickshaws are garaged on the road since he has no garage[45].

***Munilal Mahato (nee Razzaq)***, a Sardar, aged 60 years, has come to Calcutta from village Atapur Naukni district Samastipur in Bihar. At present he stays in a rented room at Belgachia. He came to Calcutta at the age of 17/18 years with his paternal uncle, Mohan Razzaq who used to work as a porter in Burrabazar, for the purpose of earning an income. He has been pulling rickshaw for the last 40 years. Swapan Kumar Roy is his rickshaw owner. Since a few months ago he became a Sardar for his owner's rickshaws. In the past, around 20 years ago, he as a puller, used to pay Rs.2.50 per day to his owner and this rate has now increased to Rs.30/- per day per rickshaw. Now, he along with his family live in Calcutta. Munilal further informs us that as a Sardar he has to take care of the rickshaws of the owner, to find out whether any rickshaw needs repairing, to collect the weekly payment from the rickshaw pullers and to hand over the money collected to the owner of the rickshaws. His owner pays him Rs.100/- per day and one rickshaw free of cost for him to pull and thereby earn an extra income out of which he is not required to pay any rent to the owner. Munilal pulls a rickshaw for 2 to 4 hours. He earns around Rs.4,000/- to Rs.5,000/- per month. His only son, now married, works elsewhere but does not pull a rickshaw. If e-rickshaw is permitted in Calcutta, Munilal is willing to drive the same[46].

***Debu Yadav***, a puller aged 60 years and hailing from village Dhunachi, district Bhagalpur, in Bihar, came to Calcutta at the age of 30 years and started pulling rickshaw of Late Budhaban Mahato, father of Sunil Mahato. He earns Rs.200 to Rs.300/- per day and has to pay Rs.30/- to his owner, Sunil Mahato at present. He has been staying with his family in a rented room at Jagatpur. He pulls a rickshaw from 8-00 a.m. to 6-00 p.m.. If hand pulled rickshaw is banned totally, he will have to seek an alternative job for a living. If government permits e-rickshaws he is willing to drive e-rickshaw[47].

***Moh. Yunus***, aged 72 years is a rickshaw owner and has 16 hand pulled rickshaws. He has been involved in this business for the last 40 years. At the age of 15/16 years Yunus came to Calcutta from village Sk. Tolilaokhan in district Motihari in Bihar along with some villagers. At first he started pulling a rickshaw, thereafter he became a Sardar and subsequently he bought 16 rickshaws from several owners. He has been a member of ABRU for a long time by paying a membership fee of Rs.10/- annually. All his pullers are Biharis. Every puller pays him Rs.30/- per day. Yunus pays Rs.400/- per month to the police in the New Market Police Station and Rs.200/- per month to the police in Taltola Police Station. Every month he earns Rs.5,000/- to Rs.6,000/-. His family is in his village and he goes home 2/3 times a year. He has two daughters (married) and four sons who are settled in Bombay. His rickshaws are garaged on the road while 6/7 pullers stay in his room at 27, Aga Mehendi Street, Kolkata[48].

***Joy Kumar Rana***, aged 40 years, hailing from village Bagmundi, in district Chhatra in Jharkhand, is a *rickshaw owner*. His father, Chetlal Rana first started this business of hand pulled rickshaw with Ramnath Shaw on the basis of an oral partnership in 1979. They started with 20 rickshaws. Joy Kumar states that in the 1970s till 1982-83 their rickshaws were allowed to be pulled all over Calcutta. His father looked after this business upto 1996 and thereafter Joy Kumar started looking after this business since mid – 1996. As regards his family Joy Kumar informs us that he has two younger brothers, and three elder sisters who are married. His two brothers are working in Hazaribagh and Chennai respectively. From 1996 to 2018 he had 46 rickshaws. But in 2019 during the disaster caused by construction undertaken by Metro Railways, most of the lanes in Bowbazar area were closed for ingress and egress as a result of which it became difficult for the pullers to pull their rickshaws in these lanes[49].

At present Joy Kumar has only 12 rickshaws running on the road. After the Covid disaster the number of rickshaw pullers has decreased and few pullers are coming from Bihar and Jharkhand. The present pullers who are pulling his rickshaws are a few Bengali hindus coming from Canning in South 24 Parganas and pullers from Gaya, Nabada and Giridih, Joy Kumar has got a rickshaw garage at 15, Sankrapara Lane, Bowbazar, Kolkata – 700012 where 8 pullers have been staying and they cook and eat in a common mess. Joy Kumar and his wife and children have been living in two rooms inside this garage. Subhas Dey is the owner and landlord of this garage. Joy Kumar states that his pullers pay him Rs.30/- per day per rickshaw and Rs.200/- per week. His rickshaws ply in College Street, Burrabazar and Sealdah. Joy Kumar earns around Rs.4,000/- per month from the rickshaw business. Joy Kumar has also got a Tata Sumo Car which he drives and picks up students from the Kendriya Vidyalaya and takes them home everyday on payment basis. For the last 7 years he has been engaged in this pull car business. He has two sons and two daughters who are all school students. Joy Kumar has been a member of All Bengal Rickshaw Union since 1999. He pays Rs.100/- annually as membership fee. The last meeting which he attended in the office of ABRU was in 2012-13. He has a rickshaw repairman from Bihar who repairs his rickshaws. Most of the repairmen hail from Vaishali and Muzaffarpur in Bihar, Joy Kumar pays Rs.400/- per day to the repairman along with free lunch everyday. The repairman works for 8 hours a day and if he works overtime for 2 to 3 hours, Joy Kumar pay him Rs.40/- per hour as overtime fee. Joy Kumar is willing to start e-rickshaws if such rickshaw is permitted by the Government[50].

***Santosh Shaw***, aged around 48 years and hailing from Benaras in U.P. is a rickshaw owner. His grandfather, late Hiralal Shaw started the business of handrickshaw during the British rule. Subsequently Santosh Shaw's father late Ramnath Shaw carried on this business. Santosh informs us that his forefathers built a temple of Goddess Durga at Durgapithuri Lane, Kolkata – 700012 and the money earned from this rickshaw business was spent for the seva (worship) of Goddess Durga since the time of his predecessors. But this temple has been destroyed by the underground digging of lanes and roads by Metro Railway. Santosh Shaw states that he has 100 rickshaws and his rickshaw pullers are hindus from Bihar and U.P. Around 20 pullers stay in his rickshaw garage at 15, Sankrapara Lane, Bowbazar, Kolkata – 700012 and they eat in a common mess. There are four repairmen who repair the rickshaws and stay in this garage. These repairmen hail from Vaishali in Bihar. Each puller pays Santosh Shaw Rs.30/- per day and Rs.200/- per week. If police arrest any puller in a petty case, Santosh pays a fine of Rs.100/- to the police[51].

Santosh Shaw also owns a jewellery shop under the name and style of "Shaw Jewellers" at 90, B.B. Ganguly Street dealing in silver and gold jewellery and artifacts. This shop was established by his predecessors seven generations ago. Santosh is a member of All Bengal Rickshaw Union. He pays Rs.380/- per day to a rickshaw repairman who works for 8 hours per day. He also provides boarding and lodging to the rickshaw repairmen. In Santosh Shaw's opinion rickshaw business has now become very costly as he has to spend more money to maintain this business but he earns less and has to face loss in this business. Finally Santosh expressed his interest in e-rickshaw[52].

The author met two rickshaw repairmen in the rickshaw garage at 15, Sankrapara Lane, Kolkata – 700012. One of them, ***Indrajit Sharma***, aged 56 years, hailing from Vaishali in Bihar, states that his father, late Hridaye Sharma was also a rickshaw craftsman who came to Calcutta prior to 1947 in search of work and he worked in Calcutta till 1980. Indrajit informs us that he learnt the repairing work from his father and has been working in this garage for the last 10 years. He first started work under Ramnath Shaw. His working hours is from 9-00 a.m. to 6-00 p.m. He gets Rs.300/- per day from the owner of this garage and the owner provides him lunch only. He has got agricultural land in his native place which is taken care of by his brothers. His son works in a call center in Calcutta[53].

***Umesh Sharma***, aged 52 years and hailing from Vaishali, in Bihar is also a rickshaw craftsman. His father, late Tarakeswar Sharma was also a rickshaw craftsman. He has been working in this garage for 4 years. His family is in Bihar. His eldest son, a graduate is looking for a job while his youngest son is reading in Class-XI and wants to join college after completing school. Out of the sale proceeds of agricultural land, he has been paying for the education of both his sons[54].

***Nagen Halder***, aged 60 years, is the only Bengali in Calcutta who knows the art of repairing and constructing a hand pulled rickshaw. Originally from Gumohowrah, he has been living in Calcutta since his birth as his father has a rented room at 1B, Jadu Mitra Lane, Kolkata – 700004. He learnt about the repair work of a rickshaw from Nathni Thakur whose native place was Muzaffarpur. Since 1973 Nagen Halder has been involved in the work of repairing and constructing a rickshaw. He first started work in the garage of Uma Shankar Pandey at 14, Ultadanga Road. For 30 years he worked in the garage of Uma Shankar Pandey. In 2019 when Uma Shankar died, Nagen Haldar started his own repairing workshop by renting another room adjacent to his room. Now he repairs the rickshaws of the owners whose rickshaws ply in this area or in the nearby area. But now he does not get work on a regular basis due to banning of rickshaws by the Government[55].

Nagen Haldar gives us some details about the construction of a hand pulled rickshaw. He uses shesham wood for constructing the round of the wheel while the inside rows of the wheel are made of salwood. The body of the rickshaw is made of ghoraneem wood. The seat and hood of the rickshaw are made by a separate man who knows the art of making them and has a shop at Shyambazar. As regards his family, Nagen Haldar tells us that he has got three daughters and one son of whom two daughters are married. His youngest daughter is a student of Class-XI while his son, aged 32 years, is a motor mechanic and works in a car garage. Nagen is willing to learn about repairing of e-rickshaw, if the government permits e-rickshaws[56].

***Raj Kumar Thakur***, aged 52 years, hailing from Vaishali in Bihar, is a rickshaw owner having 15/16 rickshaws at present which ply on the roads of north Calcutta. His paternal grandfather, and his father late Ramsagar Thakur started work as a rickshaw craftsmen. Thereafter his father bought a few rickshaws and became an owner. In the 1980s his father owned around 300 to 400 rickshaws, which used to ply on the roads of north Calcutta. After completion of his graduation from Vidyasagar College, he joined this business in the early 1990s. In the 1990s they had 80 to 90 rickshaws. At that time there were two kinds of licences for hand pulled rickshaws viz. Bengal licence and Calcutta licence. Bengal licence was issued from 1970 till 1988. In 1990 the Dum Dum Municipality stopped issuing Bengal licence[57].

Among the pullers who are now pulling Raj Kumar Thakur's rickshaws, 10/12 of them are Bihari hindus hailing from Muzaffarpur and Jharkhand, 2 are Behari muslims, and 2/3 are Bengali hindus from Barasat (North), Ghatakpur and New Town. Each puller pays him Rs.30/- per day and Rs.200/- per week. Raj Kumar has to pay Rs.150/- per month to the local police station at Shyampukur and Rs.200/- per month to the Traffic Guard at Shyambazar. He also pays Rs.100/- as fine to the police for petty cases as every month the police starts 3 to 4 petty cases involving his rickshaw pullers. Raj Kumar earns around Rs.3,000/- per month from the rickshaw business. He is a member of All Bengal Rickshaw Union and pay Rs.10/- annually as membership fee. He is interested in starting a business in e-rickshaw if government permits e-rickshaws in Calcutta[58].

***Sukul Sharma***, aged 73 years, hailing from village Pathepur, district Vaishali in Bihar, is at present a rickshaw owner cum Sardar cum rickshaw mechanic. He first came to Calcutta along with a villager, late Ajodhya Sharma who was a rickshaw owner. At that time Sukul started learning repairing work in the garage of late Jagdish Shaw and thereafter started work under Ajodhya Shaw. But after the death of Jagdish Shaw two years ago, his widow closed the rickshaw garage at 22A, Rajendra Mullick Street, Kolkata – 700007. Now Sukul has 4 rickshaws of his own and 6 rickshaws on the basis of a contract as a Sardar. He still does repair work in other rickshaw garages. The pullers pays him Rs.30/- per day and Rs.200/- per week. He pay Rs.100/- to local Girish Park Police Station per month and also he has to pay the fine for petty cases involving his rickshaws. Every month after all payments he earns Rs.2,500/- to Rs.3,000/- as income. He goes home 3 to 4 times a year and he hires labourers for the cultivating his land. He is not a member of ABRU. As regards his family he has one married daughter and four sons, of whom one son works in a furniture shop and another is a driver of a rented (OLA) car while the younger two sons are at home. Sukul Sharma is interested in e-rickshaw if it is permitted by the Government[59].

***Dr. Mohammad Iqbal***, aged 70 years, is a rickshaw owner and he is the third generation in his family carrying on this business. His grandfather, Roshan Ali was a rickshaw owner and he had 11 rickshaws which used to ply in the Park Circus area. Dr. Iqbal's father, late Abdul Rajjak, was also a rickshaw owner and he had 20 to 25 rickshaws which plyed in the Park Circus area. Dr. Iqbal has been in this business for the last 30 years. Prior to covid calamity he had 150 rickshaws. But now he has 80 rickshaws which ply in Park Circus area, Bhawanipur, Lake Market area, Ballygunge place and in Ballygunge Station Road. He has a rickshaw garage at 2C, Tiljala Road, Kolkata – 700046 where there is a rickshaw craftsman for repairing the rickshaws and the rickshaws are kept in this garage at night. Dr. Iqbal states that he himself looks after this business and he does not have any Sardar to take care of the business. Every puller pays Dr. Iqbal Rs.25/- to Rs.30/- per day[60].

Dr. Iqbal had been a President of the Rickshaw Puller's Union. This Union's office is at B.B. Ganguly Street, Kolkata. His paternal uncle, Najib Khan was the Secretary of this Union for the last 20 years. Mohammad Sharif was the treasurer of this Union. Dr. Iqbal further informs us that now his business is running in loss as many pullers left home forever after handpulled rickshaws were banned by the government and the sons of the pullers, who have grown too old to be able to pull rickshaws, are not willing to join this business as they are earning money from doing other jobs[61].

Dr. Iqbal is an Unani doctor and his chamber is

at 2C, Tiljala Road. He studied Unani medicine from the Unani Hospital at Mehedi Bagan for 3 years. He has got two daughters, one married and one studying at present, and one son who is settled in Bihar and has a medicine shop there. After Dr. Iqbal, his business in rickshaws will come to an end as none of his family members is interested to continue this business. Dr. Iqbal has never been a member of All Bengal Rickshaw Union[62].

***Debnath Kamat***, aged 50 years, hailing from village Tilayu, in district Madhubani in Bihar, has been pulling a rickshaw for many years. He first came to Calcutta at the age of 15/16 years with a man from his village. This man named Shivlal also used to pull a rickshaw in the Bhowanipur area. At first Debnath used to do household work for 2 years in some local houses in Bhowanipur for his sustinance. Thereafter he started pulling a rickshaw from 6-00 a.m. to 12-00 p.m. (afternoon) and from 4-00 p.m. to 8-00 p.m. In the past he used to earn Rs.100/- to Rs.150/- in two shifts. Now he earns around Rs.300/- to Rs.400/- per day. He pay Rs.200/- to the owner per week. Previously he used to pull the rickshaw of Sakal Roy who had a garage at Ramesh Mitra Road, Kolkata – 700025. Debnath's dera (lodging & boarding) is at 7, Harish Chatterjee Road, Kolkata – 700025. In this dera or room, another rickshaw puller and himself and one or two car drivers stay. The rent of this room is Rs.1,200/- per month and his share is Rs.300/- to Rs.400/- per month. He is a member of ABRU. He has agricultural land in his native village and he visits home twice a year, during summer and monsoon. He has his wife, one son and three daughters of whom his son, aged 20 years is working in an office in Mumbai while two of his daughters are married and the youngest one is studying in Class-X[63].

***Jaleswar Sharma***, aged 60 years, hailing from village Rusulpur Ganghasi, district Vaishali in Bihar, came to Calcutta around 40 years ago. His grandfather Jeetu Thakur and his father Fakera Sharma used to repair Fiton Carriages drawn by horses. Afterwards when this carriages were banned, his father started repairing rickshaws. Jaleswar learnt the work of repairing a rickshaw from his father and he has been staying and working in the rickshaw garage at 2C, Tiljala Road for the last 24 years. Previously he used to stay with his father at 237/Q, Maniktala Main Road, Kolkata – 700054. In the garage at 2C, Tiljala Road, Jaleswar repairs only Dr. Mohammad Iqbal's rickshaws. In the past he used to make new rickshaws. Ghoreneem wood is used to make the whole structure of the rickshaw while salwood is used for making the campus or the two rods which the puller holds and pulls the rickshaw. The seat of the rickshaw is made of coconut's skin and bichali (hay of the paddy). Tin is used to cover the body of the rickshaw and the hood and curtain of the rickshaw is made of cotton material. Previously all fittings of the rickshaw were made of brass but now the fittings are made of iron. Jaleswar further informs us that he can construct a rickshaw in 15 days. His working hours are from 7-00 a.m. to 12-30 p.m. (noon) and from 3-00 p.m. to 6-00 p.m. He is paid Rs.400/- per day by the owner of this garage and he has his food in a local hotel[64].

Jaleswar visits his home twice a year in summer and winter. He has some agricultural land in his native place. He has his wife, four daughters and two sons who are living there. If rickshaw business is banned he will have to search for an alternative work in Calcutta for survival[65].

***Swarna Singh***, has been the executive Secretary of All Bengal Rickshaw Union since 1998. He was born and brought up in Bhawanipur. His father was an ayurveda doctor and had a chamber at 9A, Padmapukur Road, Kolkata. Swarna Singh is the owner of two rickshaws which used to ply in the Bhawanipur area since 2009 to 2020. But due to want of repair his rickshaws are not in a workable condition now.[66]

***Mohammad Mukhtar***, aged 60 years, hailing from village Charghara, district Deoghar in Jharkhand, came to Calcutta 40 years ago with his maternal uncle who used to work as an assistant of a mason. Mohammad has been staying in the rickshaw garage at 28/1, Beniapukur Road and pulling a rickshaw for his living. He now earns Rs.150/- to Rs.200/- per day and pays Rs.20/- per day to the owner of the rickshaw. His family is staying in his native place. He is the only man from his village who pulls a rickshaw in Calcutta. He is interested in driving an e-rickshaw if the government permits the same[67].

***Sukkan Ram***, aged 60 years, and hailing from village Sukki, Vaishali district in Bihar, came to Calcutta in 1979 with his uncle who was a rickshaw puller and lived in the garage at 28/1, Beniapukur Road. He visits his native place after every 3 or 4 months and stays there for more than a month. Sukkan used to pull a rickshaw of Anwar Hussain's father and thereafter under his elder brother and now he pulls the rickshaw of Anwar Hussain who is the owner of this garage. Now he earns Rs.300/- to Rs.400/- per day and he pays Rs.35/- to his owner per day. He earns around Rs.2,000/- to Rs.3,000/- per month and he sends the major portion of his income to his family. He is interested in driving an e-rickshaw if the government gives permission for e-rickshaw[68].

***Bharat Yadav***, aged 48 years and hailing from village Bhalwar Chaungai, district Gaya in Bihar, came to Calcutta in 1989 and started pulling a rickshaw from 1989 till 1994 under Gamruda Shaw whose rickshaw garage is at 7, Nebubagan Lane, Kolkata– 700003. At that time he earned Rs.100/- per day and paid Rs.4/- to his owner per day. In the meantime he took formal training in driving a four wheeler car. In 1994 he got his driving licence and since then he has been driving a taxi or a private car as per availability. But when he gets no job of driving a four wheeler, he pulls a rickshaw. At present around 30 pullers have learnt driving four wheeler cars. His family lives in his native place and he visits home during monsoon for cultivating his agricultural land. He stays in the rickshaw garage at 7, Nebubagan Lane[69].

***Sarju Mahato***, aged 68 years and hailing from village Asiya, district Hazaribagh in Jharkhand is at present a rickshaw owner and he owns 85 to 86 rickshaws in Calcutta. He came to Calcutta in 1974 with his father late Gandawari Mahato who was a rickshaw puller and lived in a rickshaw garage at 1B, Radha Prasad Lane. Sarju came to Calcutta at the age of 19 and started work as a rickshaw puller under Md. Sharif who was a rickshaw owner. Sarju was a rickshaw puller for 25 to 30 years. Since 1982-83 he had been a sardar, by taking care of others' rickshaws. His rickshaws now ply throughout Calcutta wherever the pullers get passengers. Sarju further informs us that when he started purchasing rickshaws in 1996-97 the price was Rs.14,000/- to Rs.15,000/- per rickshaw which later increased to Rs.20,000/- to Rs.22,000/-. Sarju has his own rickshaw garage at 4/1/2A, Radhaprasad Lane, Kolkata – 700009. Every puller pays him Rs.30/- per day viz. Rs.200/- per week. Sarju earns Rs.12,000/- to Rs.15,000/- per month. This income is not fixed as many pullers visit home in November for the purpose of cutting crops and also in the months of June-July when paddy is cultivated. Sarju's family also live in his native place. He visits home at times. He has three sons and one daughter who are all married. His sons are doing different jobs and they are not interested in this rickshaw business[70].

Sarju Mahato has been a member of All Bengal Rickshaw Union since 1998. He pays Rs.10/- annually to the Union. He states that now no new person is coming to him for pulling a rickshaw. Every month Sarju has to pay Rs.500/- to Rs.1,000/- to five police stations viz. Manicktala, Jorabagan, Burrabazar, Bowbazar and Jorasanko Police Stations[71].

***Babuni Mahato***, aged 62 years and hailing from village Gunja in district Hazaribagh, in Jharkhand, is a rickshaw puller. He first came to Calcutta at the age of 16/17 years with his maternal uncle, Sarju Sharma. For the last 21 years Babuni has been pulling a rickshaw. He earns Rs.200/- to Rs.300/- per day and he sends Rs.1,000/- to Rs.2,000/- to his family every month. He has to pay Rs.30/- to his owner per day. His rickshaw's owner looks after the maintenance of the rickshaw as well as faces the police hazards. If e-rickshaw is permitted he is willing to drive e-rickshaw. He has less agricultural land and he visits home after every 6 months and stays there for one or two months[72].

***Arjun Razzak***, aged 45 years and hailing from village Asiya, in district Hazaribagh in Jharkhand, came to Calcutta at the age of 20 years with his elder brother, Ram Razzak who used to pull a rickshaw. Since then he has been pulling a rickshaw. He earns Rs.200/- to Rs.250/- per day and he has to pay Rs.30/- per day to the owner of the rickshaw. His family lives in his village and he has some agricultural land. He visits home to cultivate paddy in his land. His two daughters are married. He is willing to drive e-rickshaw if it is permitted by the government[73].

***Abdul Razzak*** has been pulling rickshaw for over 30 years or so. Razak came to the city as a child to join his father and send money back to his family in their village, working first as a chai-boy and moving on to pull his first rickshaw in 1979. Like the vast majority of rickshawpullers he is from Bihar, the source of the country's physical and migrant labour. He has his wife, two daughters and four sons in his village home. He lives along with 50 other rickshawwallahs in one of the city's 'dheras', a barn like building where the rickshaws are garaged at night and the pullers sleep side by side. The 'dhera' is maintained by the local Sardar or middleman, who collects rent for the vehicles, pockets his commission and pays the rest to the rickshaw owner. Razzak, unschooled and unskilled is proud of his work and scornful of any philanthropic pity. He says, "this is my livelihood. It is not inhuman. It is a long tradition. I have to do this job. I don't have skills for any other kind of more 'human' work". However he admits that he does not want his sons to follow in his footsteps. But he cannot conceive a future for himself if the ban on rickshaw pulling is implemented[74].

The foregoing elaborate discussion on the present rickshaw owners and rickshaw pullers in Calcutta goes to show that the hand pulled rickshaw business comprises of four categories of people viz.

the rickshaw owners, pullers, sardars or the middlemen who supervise the work of the rickshaw pullers on behalf of the owners on commission basis and the rickshaw craftsmen who construct new rickshaws and also repair the old rickshaws. These four categories of people involved in the hand pulled rickshaw trade are inter dependent and are indispensable to one another. Most of the hand rickshaw owners, pullers, and sardars at present are Bihari hindus as well as Bihari muslims hailing from different villages in Bihar and Jharkhand with a few Bengalis (both hindus & muslims) from the villages in South 24 Parganas or from the other outskirts of Calcutta. The rickshaw repairmen are all Bihari hindus hailing mostly from the villages in Vaishali district or Muzaffarpur district of Bihar. These rickshaw craftsmen have learnt the art of constructing new rickshaws and repairing old rickshaws from their forefathers and the same is continuing through generation after generation as a sort of family trade or occupation. Another interesting characteristic feature evident from the above discussion is that many present owners are following the footsteps of their fathers or grandfathers by continuing with the rickshaw trade while many rickshaw pullers have subsequently turned into sardars and eventually owners of the rickshaws and thereby prospering in this business. Another interesting feature is that the majority of the pullers came to Calcutta accompanied by their father or any other family member or a village neighbour who also worked as a puller in Calcutta, and who helped them in getting a job as a rickshaw puller.

But it is relevant to point out in this connection that the present generation viz. the school or college going sons and daughters of the rickshaw owners and pullers are apathetic in joining this rickshaw business. The present generation is interested in doing other jobs like jobs in call centers if they can have the basic training in computers or migrating to Mumbai and other cities of India where there is prospect for getting jobs; while some rickshaw pullers by undertaking the training of driving a four wheeler have now become drivers driving either a rented OLA or Uber or taxi or a private car. So one major question which poses a threat to the handpulled rickshaw trade is that what is the future of this business if majority of the present younger generation family members of rickshaw owners and pullers are not interested in continuing with this business as because they are now educated and some of them have received technical training for other jobs, which offer them good salary and better working conditions.

Previously the rickshaw owners and pullers who came to Calcutta in search of a living had almost no education or illiterate and had no formal training to do any job other than pulling a hand rickshaw which requires no skill or formal training but only physical strength and physical fitness. But now the scenario has changed to a great extent as most of the sons of the present rickshaw owners and pullers are now going to schools and colleges and after completing education their ambition is to search for a suitable job. A notable example is the admission of Brijesh Yadav, son of a hand rickshaw puller cum owner, Kishan Deo Yadav, to the Calcutta Medical College as his ambition is to become a doctor. He is now appearing for 3rd year final MBBS Examination. While Neha Yadav the only daughter of Kishan Deo Yadav, is a 3rd year final B.Com. student in Deshbandhu Women's College at Rashbehari Avenue. She is aspiring to become an IAS Officer and she is taking preparation for appearing in the UPSC Examination. Yet the fact remains that at present around 2000 hand pulled rickshaws are still plying on the various lanes, bye-lanes and roads throughout the city of Calcutta although there are still now 6000 hand rickshaws in Calcutta unofficially.

***Notes and References***


1. Thomas, Dr. T.H., 'Rickshaws in Calcutta', a report in association with Unnayan, AIIPH (36/1A Garcha Road, Calcutta-19), February, 1981, p. 27.
2. Thomas, Dr. T.H., 'Rickshaws in Calcutta', a report, op. cit. pp 19-20.
3. Personal survey of the rickshaw garages in Calcutta and interaction with the rickshaw pullers in Calcutta made by the author in the year 2022.
4. Personal survey of the rickshaw stands in Calcutta made by the author in 2022 & 2023.
5. Thomas, Dr. T.H., 'Rickshaw in Calcutta' a report in association with Unnayan, op.cit. p. 22.

5a. Thomas, Dr. T.H., Rickshaws in Calcutta, a report in association with Unnayan, op. cit. p. 22.

6. Thomas, D.T.H., 'Rickshaws in Calcutta', a report in association with Unnayan, op.cit. p. 22.
7. Thomas, Dr. T.H., 'Rickshaws in Calcutta', a report, op.cit. p. 23.
8. Thomas, Dr. T.H., 'Rickshaws in Calcutta', a report, op.cit. p. 24.
9. Thomas, Dr. T.H. 'Rickshaws in Calcutta', a report, op.cit. p. 24.
10. Thomas, Dr. T.H., 'Rickshaws in Calcutta', a report, op.cit. pp. 22-23.
11. The Modern Review, Vol XLIX, "Bhadrak Rickshaw pullers" (Notes), Calcutta, May, 1931, p. 618.
12. Personal survey of the rickshaw garages in north and south Calcutta made by the author in the year 2022.

13. Personal Interview of Bablu Haldar, Sunil Sardar & Sona Mondal taken by the author on 30.10.2022 at Gariahat Road, Kolkata.
14. Personal Interview of Jamiruddin Jamal, Sk. Nazim & Moh. Tohid taken by the author on 13.11.2022 at Lindsay Street, Kolkata.
15. Personal Interview of Nandu Shaw, Misrilal Yadav, Sudhan Das & Budar Das taken by the another on 13.11.2022 at 10, Cornfield Raod, Kolkata.
16. Personal Interview of Prakash Shaw taken by the author on 20.11.2022 at 7, Nebubagan Lane, Kolkata – 700003.
17. Personal Interview of Mahesh Yadav & Sudeswar Yadav taken by the another on 22.11.2022 outside the rickshaw garage at 7, Nebubaan Lane, Kolkata – 700003.
18. Personal Interview of Haricharan Yadav taken by the author on 20.22.2022 at the rickshaw stand at Shyambazar.
19. Personal Interview of Mukhtar Ali taken by the author at his office at 56, Beck Bagan Row, Park Circus, Kolkata – 700017 on 29.11.2022.
20. Personal Interview of Anwar Hussain taken by the author at his rickshaw garage at 28/1, Beniapukur Road, Kolkata on 11.12.2022.
21. Personal Interview of Kishan Deo Yadav taken by the author on 12.12.2022 at his rickshaw garage at 219/A1, Picnic Garden Road, Kolkata – 700039.
22. Personal Interview of Kishan Deo Yadav taken by the author, op.cit.
23. Personal Interview of Kishan Deo Yadav taken by the author, op.cit.
24. Personal Interview of Kishan Deo Yadav taken by the author, op.cit.
25. Personal Interview of Kishan Deo Yadav taken by the author, op.cit. & Personal Interview of Kishan Deo Yadav taken by the author in the office of All Bengal Rickshaw Union at 51, Chittaranjan Avenue, on 02.04.2024.

26. Personal Interview of Tenny Sharma taken by the author on 12.12.2022 at 219/A1, Picnic Garden Raod, Kolkata – 700039.
27. Personal Interview of Parameswar Sharma taken by the author of 12.12.2022 at 219/A1, Picnic Garden Raod, Kolkata – 700039.
28. Personal Interview of Dhurup Shaw taken by the author on 12.12.2022 at his garage at 40P, Dr. G.S. Bose Road, Kolkata – 700039.
29. Personal Interview of Dhurup Shaw taken by the author, op.cit.
30. Personal Interview of Ramdhani Sharma taken by the author on 13.12.2022 in his rickshaw garage at 236, B.B. Ganguly Street, Kolkata - 7000`12.
31. Personal Interview of Ramdhani Sharma taken by the author, op.cit.
32. Personal Interview of Ramdhani Sharma taken by the author, op.cit.
33. Personal Interview of Ramdhani Sharma, op.cit.
34. Personal Interview of Ramdhani Sharma, op.cit.
35. Personal Interview of Ramdhani Sharma, op.cit.
36. Personal Interview of Ramdhani Sharma, op.cit.
37. Personal Interviews of Moh. Israil & Moh. Salem taken by the author on 13.12.2022 at 236, B.B. Ganguly Street, Kolkata – 700012 in the rickshaw garage of Ramdhani Sharma.
38. Personal Interviews of Ram Ekbal Sharma & Chandreswar Sharma taken by the author in the garage at 236, B.B. Ganguly Street, Kolkata – 700012 on 13.12.2022.
39. Personal Interview of Kashinath Paul taken by the author on 23.12.2022 at 236, B.B. Ganguly Street, Kolkata - 700012.
40. Personal Interview of Swapan Kumar Roy taken by the author on 23.12.2022 at 236, B.B. Ganguly Street, Kolkata - 700012.
41. Personal Interview of Swapan Kumar Roy taken by the

author on 27.12.2022 at 21/2A, Mahendra Goswami Lane, Kolkata – 700006.

42. Personal Interview of Swapan Kumar Roy taken by the author, op.cit.
43. Personal Interview of Tulsi Shaw taken by the author on 27.12.2022 at 21/2A, Mahendra Goswami Lane, Kolkata – 700006.
44. Personal Interview of Sanjay Yadav taken by the author on 27.12.2022 at the rickshaw stand at C.R. Avenue, Kolkata.
45. Personal Interview of Rajkumar Ghosh taken by the author on 27.12.2022 at 28A, Nanda Mullick Lane, Kolkata - 700006.
46. Personal Interview of Munilal Mahato taken by the author on 27.12.2022 in the garage of Swapan Roy.
47. Personal Interview of Debu Yadav taken by the author on 29.12.2022 at 130, Ramdeo Sarkar Street, Kolkata – 700006.
48. Personal Interview of Moh. Yunus, taken by the author on 23.01.2023 at 27, Aga Mehendi Street, Kolkata.
49. Personal Interview of Joy Kumar Rana taken by the author on 24.01.2023 at 15, Sankrapara Lane, Bowbazar, Kolkata – 700012.
50. Personal Interview of Joy Kumar Rana taken by the author, op.cit.
51. Personal Interveiw of Santosh Shaw taken by the author on 28.01.2023 in his shop "Shaw Jewellers" at 90, B.B. Ganguly Street, Kolkata – 700012.
52. Personal Interview of Santosh Shaw taken by the author, op. cit.
53. Personal Interview of Indrajit Sharma taken by the author on 28.01.2023 at 15, Sankrapara Lane, Kolkata – 700012.
54. Personal Interview of Umesh Sharma taken by the author on 28.01.2023 at 15, Sankrapara Lane, Kolkata – 700012.
55. Personal Interview of Nagen Thakur taken by the

author on 04.02.2023 at 1B, Jadu Mitra Lane, Kolkata – 700004.

56. Personal Interview of Nagen Haldar taken by the author on 04.02.2023 at 1B, Jadu Mitra Lane, Kolkata – 700004.
57. Personal Interview of Raj Kumar Thakur taken by the author on 04.02.2023 at 1B, Jadu Mitra Lane, Kolkata – 700004.
58. Personal Interview of Raj Kumar Thakur taken by the author, op. cit.
59. Personal Interview of Sukul Sharma taken by the author on 11.02.2023 at 22A, Rajendra Mullick Street, Kolkata – 700007.
60. Personal Interveiw of Dr. Mohammad Iqbal taken by the author at Balaram Bose Ghat Road, rickshawstand on 23.07.2023.
61. Personal Interveiw of Dr. M. Iqbal taken by the author, op. cit.
62. Personal Interview of Dr. M. Iqbal taken by the author on 25.07.2023 at 2/C, Tiljala Road, Kolkata.
63. Personal Interview of Debnath Kamat taken by the author on 23.07.2023 at Balaram Bose Ghat Road's rickshaw stand, Kolkata.
64. Personal Interview of Jaleswar Sharma taken by the author on 25.07.2023 at 2C, Tiljala Road, Kolkata – 700046.
65. Personal Interview of Jaleswar Sharma taken by the author, op. cit.
66. Personal Interview of Swarna Singh taken by the author in the office of ABRU on 10.12.2022.
67. Personal Interview of Moh. Mukhtar taken by the author on 10.12.2022 at 28/1, Beniapukur Raod, Kolkata.
68. Personal Interview of Sukkan Ram taken by the author on 10.08.2023 at 28/1, Beniapukur Road, Kolkata.
69. Personal Interview of Bharat Yadav taken by the author on 20.11.2022 at 7, Nebubagan Lane, Kolkata – 700003.

70. Personal Interview of Sarju Mahato taken by the author on 05.01.2023 at 4/1/2A, Radhaprasad Lane, Kolkata – 700009.
71. Personal Interview of Sarju Mahato taken by the author, op. cit.
72. Personal Interview of Babuni Mahato taken by the author on 05.01.2023.
73. Personal Interview of Arjun Razzak taken by the author on 05.01.2023.
74. ***The Statesman*** newspaper, '8th day', 10th December, 2006, Calcutta.

# Chapter V

## Laws relating to Rickshaw Trade and Litigations

The British Government passed *the **Calcutta Hackney Carriage Act**, 1919 (Bengal Act 1 of 1919)* in order to regulate the trade of any wheeled vehicle drawn by horses, palanquins and hand pulled rickshaws plying for hire in Calcutta. According to the provisions contained in section 4(8) of this Act, rickshaw means a two wheeled vehicle for the conveyance of passengers which is drawn by a man or men and includes a three wheeled vehicle, for the conveyance of passengers, ordinarily known as cycle-rickshaw which is actuated by a man by means of a pedal-cycle mechanism. Section 4(1) of this Act defines a bearer of rickshaw as a person employed to draw or pull a rickshaw[1].

Chapter VIII sections 70 and 70A of the Calcutta Hackney Carriage Act, 1919 deal with the rules and regulations regarding the rickshaws. As per the provisions of this Act every hand pulled rickshaw has to be registered and a licence will be issued from the office of the Registering Officer, provided that the Registering Officer may cancel or suspend for such period, as he thinks fit, the registration of a rickshaw if in his opinion the type of the rickshaw has been so altered as to render it different from that in respect of which registration was made. In any area included in Calcutta under clause (b) of Section 2, the functions of the Registering Officer shall be performed by an officer appointed by the Commissioners of the Municipality comprising such area and the said officer shall forward to the Deputy Commissioner of Police referred to subsection 1 of Section 6 all papers relating to registration for record after they have been duly dealt with[2].

Section 70A (inserted by West Bengal Act, 22 of 1980) deals with unlicensed rickshaws. Section 70A(1) provides that if any rickshaw, other than a cycle rickshaw, is used as such, without having any license under this Act, the owner of such rickshaw shall be liable to a fine not exceeding five hundred rupees but subject to a minimum of fifty rupees and in default of payment of fine, to simple imprisonment for a period, not exceeding three months. Any police officer or any person duly authorized by the Commissioner of Police in that behalf may seize such rickshaw and produce the same before the Magistrate and the Magistrate shall, in addition to the imposition of fine, order confiscation of the rickshaw. Sub-Section 2 of Section 70A provides that rickshaws confiscated under sub-section 1 shall be destroyed in such manner as the State Government may by general order direct. Subsection 3 of Section 70A states that a police officer or a person duly authorized by the Commissioner of Police in that behalf may seize any rickshaw without having a licence under this Act and found in the public thoroughfare, with or without its owner or the owner of which is unknown as the whereabouts of the owner of which cannot be ascertained with reasonable diligence and produce the same before the nearest Magistrate having jurisdiction and the Magistrate shall pass an order for interim custody of the rickshaw. Under the provisions of sub-section 4 of Section 70A the Magistrate shall by proclamation, make a declaration to the effect that the said rickshaw shall be confiscated and destroyed on the expiry of a period not exceeding 30 days from the date of issue of the proclamation unless the owner or the person in possession of the rickshaw appears before him and satisfies that the rickshaw was neither used nor intended to be used for carrying passengers or goods in a public thoroughfare till a licence under this Act was granted by the Registering Officer[3].

In Chapter IX, section 71, the State Government has been conferred power to make by-laws for carrying out the provisions of Calcutta Hackney Carriage Act, 1919, such as regulating the examination and qualification of bearers of rickshaws and the conditions under which they may be employed, specifying the description or other things to be used in rickshaws, the dimensions and colour of rickshaws and prescribing the conditions in which the rickshaws shall be kept, and prescribing the fees to be paid for registration of rickshaws as well as the fares to be paid for the hire of rickshaws. Section 72 of this Act provides for penalty for infringement of the by-laws. Whoever infringes any by law made under this Act shall be liable to a fine not exceeding twenty rupees and in default of payment of fine, to simple imprisonment for a period not exceeding ten days[4].

Chapter IX section 77 of the Calcutta Hackney Carriage Act, 1919, provides that property left in a rickshaw has to be deposited in the nearest police station to the Officer-in-Charge if the said property is left by any passenger in a rickshaw and is not claimed by the owner thereof. The said officer shall forthwith enter in a book to be kept for that purpose, the description of such property, the name and address of the bearer who brings it, the day and time when it was brought and the name and address of the owner of the rickshaw in which the said property has been left and the register number of such rickshaw and shall grant a receipt for the same. The said officer shall also send a copy of such entry to the Registering Officer. Section 78 of the said Act, states that the rickshawpuller shall be liable to pay a fine not exceeding Rs.50/- and in default of payment of fine, to simple imprisonment for a period not exceeding 14 days, if the bearer of the rickshaw fails to deposit the property left in the rickshaw as prescribed in section 77. Section 79 of the said Act, provides for return of the property entered under Section 77, to the person who proves to the satisfaction of the Commissioner of Police or such other police officer, not below the rank of the Inspector, that the same belonged to him, on payment of all costs incurred, together with such reasonable sum to the person who brought the same as the Commissioner or such other officer may determine. But if within six months from the date of such deposit no person satisfies the Commissioner or such other officer that he is the owner of the property, the Commissioner may cause the property to be sold or otherwise disposed of and the proceeds, after deducting therefrom the expenses, together with a reasonable sum to the bearer shall be credited and applied in the same manner as fees and fines realized under this Act[5].

It is interesting and relevant to note in this connection that the British government created a *Public Vehicles Department* comprising of two branches, one for motor vehicles and the other for the hackney carriages. This was a new department of the Calcutta Police opened for the purpose of issuing licence to the hackney carriages and rickshaws and for supervising and controlling the trade of hackney carriages and handpulled rickshaws. This fact is evident from two letters, one written by the Hon'ble Mr. J.H. Kerr, Chief Secretary to the Government of Bengal, to the Secretary to the Government of India, Home Department and the other written by Hon'ble Mr. J.H. Kerr to the Commissioner of Police.

The Hon'ble Mr. J.H. Kerr, Chief Secretary to the Government of Bengal, dated May 1919, wrote to the Secretary to the Government of India, Home Department, "I am directed to refer to my letter No. 5 P.J.-D, dated 22nd April, 1919, asking for sanction to the creation of the posts of a Superintendent of Police and an Assistant Commissioner of police for the new department of the Calcutta Police to be called the Public Vehicles Department comprising of the hackney carriages and the motor vehicles branches. The control of the former, as reported in that letter, is to be transferred under the provisions of the Calcutta Hackney Carriage Act, 1919 from the Calcutta Corporation to the Calcutta Police. It now transpires that in expectation of a speedy settlement of the question, the corporation has made no provision for hackney carriage branch in their budget of the current year, ..... I am accordingly to request that orders on my letter of 22nd April, 1919 cited above may be passed without any avoidable delay[6]".

In another letter addressed to the Commissioner of Police, Calcutta, the Hon'ble Mr. J.H. Kerr, wrote, "with reference to your letter no. 8968G-46-13, dated 13th December, 1918, I am directed to convey sanction to the taking over by the Calcutta Police of the control of hackney carriages from the Calcutta Corporation, as provided in the Calcutta Hackney Carriage Act, 1919 and to the creation of a Public Vehicles Department comprising two branches, one for motor vehicles and the other for hackney carriages, with a Deputy Commissioner of Police of the rank of Superintendent of Police, in general charge of the department and an Assistant Commissioner of Police in subordinate control of each other, together with a staff of two Inspectors, five sub-inspectors, seven head constables, twenty constables, twelve clerks, two duftries and two peons, at an estimated annual cost, including the cost of accommodation of the executive force of Rs.79,564-6 recurring and Rs.1,908/- non-recurring as detailed in the accompanying statement. Sanction is also accorded to the conversion of the *Fenwick Bazar Police building* in Corporation Street into *the headquarters of the department* which will provide accommodation for the office, the residence of the Deputy Commisioner and residential quarters for the two Assistant Commissioners and three other officers. The existing staff of the motor vehicles branch of your office including Asst. Commissioner of Police in Charge of the branch, will merge in the establishment sanctioned above, subject to the confirmation by the secretary of State. The Government of India has been pleased to sanction appointments of the Deputy Commissioner of Police and the Addl. Asst. Commissioner of Police. The Accountant, General, Bengal, has been informed[7]".

It transpires from a letter dated May, 1919 that Inspector, *Mr. J. Woolley* was appointed as *Assistant Commissioner of Police for the new Hackney Carriage Department.* Mr. R. Clerke, Esq. Commissioner of

Police, Calcutta, wrote to the Chief Secretary to the Government of Bengal in May 1919, "with reference to the Government order No. 77, P.J. dated the 27th instant sanctioning the control of hackney carriages being taken over by the Calcutta Police from the Calcutta Corporation and also the proposals submitted by me in connection with the working of the new Hackney Carriage Act, I have the honour to state that I have addressed the Legislative Department asking that the Act may be brought into effect from 1st July, 1919, I beg to recommend that 2nd grade Inspector *Mr. J. Woolley* who was in accordance with Government order No.637 P.J. dated 25th February, 1919, placed on deputation in connection with the establishment of the new Hackney Carriage Department, may be appointed as *Assistant Commissioner of Police of that Department* with effect from 1st July, 1919 and necessary notification be issued in the Calcutta Gazette[8]".

At the instance of the Commissioner of Police, Calcutta, *Mr. J. Mulcahy*, M.B.E., Officiating Deputy Commissioner of Police, Calcutta was appointed to be *Registering Officer* for the purpose of Section 6(1) of the Calcutta Hackney Carriages Act, 1919 (Bengal Act 1 of 1919)[9].

On 9th May, 1932, Mr. J. Woolley, officiating Deputy Commissioner of Police, Calcutta was appointed the Registering Officer for the purpose of Calcutta Hackney Carriage Act[9a].

It transpires from a notification by the Deputy Commissioner of Police, Hackney Carriage Department that "notice was given that the *annual registration of rickshaws* will commence on 1st day of October, 1919. Licence will only be granted for comfortable, roomy and easy running vehicles capable of seating two persons. The rickshaw shall comply with the following conditions:- The body of the rickshaw shall be sound and clean and all boards strong, properly secured and painted. The wheels shall be rubber tyred, strong and sound, so as to run true and without rattling or shaking and shall be protected by properly fitted splash boards. The springs shall be made of good metal, properly riveted and free from rust. The iron support at the back shall be properly curved and securely fixed at each side strong and of sound metal and free from rust. The shafts shall be of sound wood, securely fixed and furnished at the fore ends with ring shaped metal supports and connected by a collision guard. The hood, apron cushions, backrest and arm rests shall be made of and covered with good Khaki coloured cloth in good condition and clean[10]".

"Owners are particularly directed to note the colour which must be strictly adhered to, as no matter how good the condition of the rickshaw may be, it will not be registered, unless it is of the proper colour, body and wheels must be of one colour – dark blue with thin red lining. Authorised colour can be seen at the office of the Registering Officer, Corporation Street. No fancy work such as dragon, flowers, birds and animals are to be painted on any part of the rickshaw. Owners are strongly advised to have all their rickshaws thoroughly overhauled and done up by a competent coach builder before bringing them for registration so that they may run for the year with the ordinary repairs without breaking down. This will prove cheaper in the end for the owners. Old rickshaws that are not sound enough to run for a reasonable time without repairs will not be registered, rickshaws found altogether unfit will be punch marked with the letter 'C'. Owners are also directed to pay particular attention to rickshaw lamps. The same patterned lamps as used by Hackney Carriages must be carried on all rickshaws. Pattern may be seen at the office of the Registering Officer. Lamp brackets should be made of strong metal securely fixed so as not to shake or rattle and must be made so as to fit the lamp. Any person who is desirous of registering a rickshaw shall appear before the Registering Officer or his deputy in person, failing which no licence will be granted[11]".

On 6th January, 1932, L.H. Colson, the Commissioner of Police, Calcutta, with the previous sanction of the Governor-in-Council, made the following rules for the purpose of regulating traffic in the streets and public places of Calcutta and its suburbs:- "(1) All hand carts, rickshaws and other slow moving vehicles shall keep as close as possible to the extreme left hand side of the road or street...... they shall keep in one line only and the drivers shall not attempt to pass one another." (2) "Every hand cart shall carry a lamp suspended from the aixle midway between the wheels and exhibiting a white light visible within reasonable distance both in front and in rear". (3) "All vehicles while loading and unloading shall keep in a single line parallel to and close to the Kerb". (4) "No hand carts shall proceed along Chowringhee Road from Dhurrumtolla Street to Circular Road during the hours of 9.00 a.m. to 11.00 a.m. and 4.00 p.m. to 12 midnight. (5) "No vehicle shall remain standing for any period on any of the streets within Sir Stuart Hogg Market area" (6) "Rickshaws shall proceed direct in the Railway Station (Howrah Station) and shall be parked under the directions of the Railway Police." (7) "No hand cart of any description shall proceed along Clive Street or Clive Row during the period 9.00 a.m. to 6.00 p.m. as Clive Row shall be treated as one way traffic street in which traffic may only proceed South." (8) "In the Outram Ghat area rickshaws for hire upto 12 in number shall park on the east side of Madan Street facing, south and north of the junction of Meredith Street." (9) "In Baby Pearl Theatre, rickshaws for hire upto 10 in number shall park in rear of the park for Hackney Carriages. But in all other places of public amusement like at Albion Theatre, Alfred Theatre, Corinthian Theatre at Dharmotolla Street, Cornwallis Theatre (Natya Mandir), the Chitra Theatre at Cornwallis Street, Elphinstone Picture Palace at Chowringhcc Place, Empire Theatre at Chowringhee Place, Jupitar Cinema at Chittaranjan Avenue, Minerva Theatre at Beadon Street, Natya Niketan Theatre at Raja Raj Kissen Street, the National Bioscope at Watgunge Street, Opera House at Lindsay Street, the Plaza at Chowringhee Road, Ripon Theatre at Machuabazar Street, Star Threatre at Cornwallis Street, Madan Theatre at Corporation Street, no rickshaw but only hackney carriages for hire were permitted, to park on a single line[12]".

***The Hackney Carriage By-laws*** were amended and published *under Notification No.1084M. dated 31st March, 1920.* Though the Deputy Commissioner of Police, Public Vehicles Department, on 25th July, 1932 did not consider the grounds put forward by Messrs. Leslie & Hinds, Solicitors on behalf of Messrs Hoo Aik & Co. in support of the one seater "Hongkong Rickshaw", strong enough for approaching the Government to alter the existing rules regarding rickshaws[13], Mr. B.R. Sen, Esq. I.C.S., Addl. Deputy Secretary to the Government of Bengal, Police Department, forwarded to the Commissioner of Police, Calcutta on 30th September, 1932, a copy of the petition from Messrs Hoo Aik &

Company of 67, China Street, Rangoon regarding plying of one seater rickshaws in Calcutta. He also stated therein that there was no objection to such rickshaws plying in the city. He accordingly requested the Commissioner of Police to suggest suitable amendments to the by-law 13 of the by-laws published under notification no.1084 dated 31st March, 1920 so as to make their use legal[14]. Accordingly the Commissioner of Police forwarded to the Chief Secretary, Government of Bengal, the amendments to the by laws of the Calcutta Hackney Carriage Act in order to permit the use of one seater rickshaws within the city and suburbs of Calcutta and the Municipality of Howrah[15].

In the redraft of by-law no.13, paragraph 1, there shall be *two classes of rickshaws* of patterns fixed by the Commissioner of Police with the approval of the local government. Thus the expressions 'two' and 'patterns' underlined in the re-draft were substituted for the expression 'one' and a 'pattern' so as to provide for the plying for hire of one-seater rickshaws in Calcutta, in addition to the two seater rickshaws already in use. As per new Rule 23(4) of the bylaws the rates and fares to be paid for one seater rickshaws was fixed as follows :- (1) 1½ annas for any distance within 1 mile, (2) 1½ annas for every mile for any distance exceeding 1 mile, (3) 3 annas for any time within and not exceeding 1 hour and (4) 1½ annas for every hour a part of an hour beyond 1 hour. The by law No. 25(1) was also amended to provide that the carrying capacity of all rickshaws shall be fixed by the Commissioner of Police and the maximum number of passengers a rickshaw was licensed to carry shall be clearly painted on the vehicle in a conspicuous position in a manner approved by the Commissioner of Police. The fare for two seater rickshaws were fixed as follows : (1) 3 annas for any distance not exceeding 1 mile, (2) 3 annas for every mile, (3) 6 annas for any time not exceeding one hour, and (4) 3 annas for every hour or part of an hour beyond one hour[16].

The final Notification No.871 P1 dated 27th February, 1933 regarding one seater rickshaws was published in the Calcutta Gazette of 2nd March, 1933[17].

It further transpires from the proceedings of the Government of Bengal, Police department that "in exercise of the power conferred by clause (b) of Section 2 of the Calcutta Hackney Carriage Act, 1919 (Bengal Act 1 of 1919), the Governor-in-Council is pleased to include in Calcutta for the purpose of this Act the following municipalities, which are situated in the vicinity of Calcutta namely – Howrah, Tollygunge, South Dum Dum, Baranagore, South Suburban Bally, Kamarhati and Garden Reach[18].

In May, 1936 at the instance of the Commissioner of Police, Mr. J. Woolley, officiating Deputy Commissioner of Police Calcutta was again appointed the *Registering Officer* for the purpose of the Calcutta Hackney Carriage Act vice Mr. E.H. Le Brocq. with effect from 29th May, 1936[19].

It is relevant to note that with regard to the question of registration of rickshaws in the name of the owners, sometimes the Registering Officer faced difficulties when rickshaws were registered in the names of minors and pardanashin ladies[20].

In 1929-30 (from 01.04.29 to 31.03.30) the total number of rickshaws registered according to municipalities under the Calcutta Corporation was 2205[21]. In 1930-31 the total number of rickshaws registered according to municipalities under the Calcutta Corporation was 2301[22].

From the ***Calcutta Gazette*** *dated 24.12.1965* (Home Department, Transport) it is evident that in exercise of the powers conferred by sub-section (1) of section (4) of the West Bengal Traffic Regulation Act, 1965, the Governor made the following order:- "No rickshaw shall ply or remain standing between 8.00 a.m. and 8.00 p.m. on the roads, streets and thoroughfare or portions thereof falling within the jurisdiction of the Commissioner of Police, Calcutta as specified in the scheduled appended hereto on any day which is not a Sunday or a holiday under the Negotiable Instruments Act, 1881.

**The schedule :**

Roads, streets and thoroughfare or portions thereof:

1) Bentinck Street, (2) Canning Street, (3) Rabindra Sarani – on the portion between Canning Street and Lalbazar Street. This order came into effect on 30.12.1965[22a].

**Ban on hand pulled rickshaws in Calcutta**

As early as 1988 the then *Chief Minister of West Bengal, Mr. Jyoti Basu* took a move to ban hand-pulled rickshaws. But he was forced to abandon the project as senior leaders of the then Janata Party, Mr. George Fernandes and Mr. Lalu Prasad, came to the city and held rallies espousing the cause of the rickshawpullers. Mr. Fernandes met Mr. Basu and the drive against hand-pulled rickshaws fizzled out[23].

*Mr. Buddhadeb Bhattacharjee*, the next Chief Minister of West Bengal after Jyoti Basu, also opined, "It is inhuman for a man to carry another man. Moreover hand pulled rickshaws are still an unfortunate symbol of the city to many foreigners as are its beggars and shanties. This has to change[24]". **The Statesman** Newspaper further reported, "The Chief Minister Buddhadeb Bhattacharjee is all set to ban man-drawn rickshaws and palanquins in the city. Tomorrow (viz. on July 30, 2006) the Government will table the Calcutta Hackney Carriage Amendment Bill, 2006 in the Assembly. The amendment to the original Hackney Carriage Act of 1919 calls for a complete ban on man-drawn rickshaws and palanquins[25]".

On 4th December, 2006, ***Calcutta Hackney Carriage Amendment Bill*** was passed by the State Assembly. This was the culmination of 15 months of debate since Chief Minister, Buddhadeb Bhattacharjee announced the abolition of the century-old trade on 15th August, 2005. "The new Bill will see the trade gradually phased out and promises rehabilitation for the men involved. The role of car parking attendant is one role that has been mooted". Mr. Bhattacharjee said," We must agree on one point - in the 21st century it is not right for a human being to pull another human being ......... This is a shame for our city and state. We should have done this much earlier." While the ban was imposed on humanitarian grounds, it is also part of a wider campaign to improve the city's poor global image[26].

Mr. Buddhadeb Bhattacharjee offered a rehabilitation package for handpulled rickshaw-pullers and compensation for those unable to accept rehabilitation package. 100 rickshawpullers would be engaged to collect a parking fee from each of 20 parking zones in the city. The mayor and city Municipal Commissioner were also informed. The Chief Minister agreed that there were 5937 registered rickshaws[27].

The Kolkata Municipal Corporation stopped the

renewal or issuance of licences to rickshaw pullers across the city, after the State Government passed the Calcutta Hackney Carriage Act Bill in the State Assembly in 2006. In 2006 around 18,000 handpulled rickshaws were rendered illegal. However as instructed by the State Government, no action was taken by the Kolkata Police against the rickshaw pullers, until an alternative plan was ready for implementation. According to initial planning 20 parking lots had to be identified for providing work to at least 2000 rickshawpullers. An idea to pay Rs.1,00,000/- as compensation to the licenced rickshaws was also mooted by the State Government. The State Government had reportedly asked the Kolkata Municipal Corporation to facilitate the process by ensuring that self help groups formed by the rickshaw pullers be given priority in getting licences. However no action seems to have come of it. A new model of rickshaw called 'Dipbahan' was designed by an IIT Guwahati scientist, Mr. Amarendra Das as a possibile solution for replacing the old traditional ones. The State agricultural department, headed by Mr. Kamal Guha in 2005 ordered for ten such rickshaws to ply in Dinhata. But these rickshaws were never popularised in Kolkata as an alternative for the hand pulled ones. Confirming that no licence had been issued or renewed for hand pulled rickshaws in the city since 2006, Mayor, Mr. Bikash Ranjan Bhattacharya said, "Alternative proposals like engaging these rickshawpullers as parking attendants, setting up self help groups or imparting vocational training were mooted, but the options were shot down by the Unions[27a]".

Thus the ***Calcutta hackney Carriage (Amendment) Act***, was passed by the West Bengal legislature and with the assent of the Governor this amended act was first published in the Kolkata Gazette of 13th February, 2007. In the preamble to the principal Act, the words "and palanquins and to make certain provision with regard to rickshaws shall be omitted. In section 4 of the principal act clause (1), clause 7, and clause 8 dealing with palanquin and rickshaw shall be omitted. Chapter VII dealing with palanquins and chapter VIII dealing with rickshaws were also omitted by this amendment. In subsection 1 of Section 71 of the principal Act in clauses (a), (c), (f), (g), (i) and (m) the wards and bearers of palanquins and rickshaws shall be committed. In section 77 of the Principal Act, in the marginal note the words, 'palanquin or rickshaw' shall be omitted. In sub-section (1) of Section 77 the words 'palanquin or rickshaw' shall be omitted, and the words "or bearer thereof, as the case may be" shall be omitted and in clause (b) the words 'or bearer' shall be omitted and in clause (d) the words "palanquin or rickshaw" wherever they occur shall be omitted. In section 78 of the Principal Act, the words "or bearer" shall be omitted and the words "palanquin or rickshaw shall be omitted. In the proviso to section 79 of the Principal Act, the words "or bearer" shall be omitted. This amended Act is also known as West Bengal Act XXXV of 2006[28].

According to the provisions contained in Section 47 of Police Regulations, Calcutta, 1968 (Section 3, Bengal Act, III 1866, section 9, Bengal Act IV of 1866), the Police cannot detain rickshaws and hackney carriages at sections or sub-sections to ensure the appearance of the driver in court to answer the charge brought against him. In such a case, bail shall be immediately granted. In the event of the accused being unable to furnish bail, intimation shall be sent to the owner of the vehicle with the request that the vehicle be taken charge of as soon as possible[29].

Mr. Subroto Bandyopadhyay, is the officer-in-charge of the Hackney Carriage department, of the Kolkata Police located below the Vidyasagar Setu. There is a dumping ground adjacent to his office for the unauthorised handpulled rickshaws together with cycle rickshaws and handpulled carts which have been confiscated by the police. Mr. Subroto Bandyopadhyay informed the author that handpulled rickshaws are still under the control of the Kolkata Police and now there are 20 handpulled rickshaws dumped in this dumping ground. Last on 31.12.2021 one handrickshaw was dumped. The reason for dumping is unauthorised rickshaws viz the rickshaw is not registered or has no licence or there is no name plate on the rickshaw. He further stated that the total numbers of handpulled rickshaws in Calcutta, according to the official records, is 5937. Any type of violence committed by a non-motorised vehicle is dealt by the concerned police station which collects the fine for petty cases. But Hackney Carriage department does not collect any fee or fine. He finally informed us that after 6 months of dumping of handrickshaws a notification is published in the Police Gazette No. T.P./37 dated 24.11.2021 and all dumped rickshaws including other carriages are e-auctioned by the auction department at Lal Bazar. The rickshaws are broken and auctioned part by part. But if any puller can show a valid licence, then the Hackney Carriage department will return the rickshaw, dumped in the dumping ground, to him. Mr. Bandyopadhyay stated that his office staff comprising of 14 homeguards sometimes do joint raids on handpulled rickshaws when the local traffic guard of a particular area seeks their help[29a].

**Litigations filed against the Calcutta Hackney Carriage Act, 1919 and the Calcutta Hackney Carriage (Amendment) Act, 2007 :**

It transpires from a lawyer's letter dated 18.09.1987 that a writ application under Article 226 of the Constitution of India was preferred in the High Court, Calcutta against the Commissioner of Police and Deputy Commissioner of Police (Traffic) cum Registering Officer under the Calcutta Hackney Carriage Act, 1919, Lalbazar, Calcutta -1. This application was filed by Ram Swarup Tanti and 21 others as a *Court application on 18.09.1987* challenging certain provisions of the abovementioned Act, 1919 and also certain irregularities regarding granting of new bearer's licences and renewal of old bearer's licences as also other illegalities on the part of the police authorities. After hearing His Lordship Hon'ble Mr. Justice Bhagabati Prasad Banerjee was pleased to direct the police authorities to consider the application of the petitioners nos. 1 to 2, in respect of issuance of new bearer's licence and renewal of old bearer's licences as the case may be[30].

On 18th March, 1998 a writ application numbered as *W.P. No.3262 of 1998* (All Bengal Rickshaw Union & Ors. Vs. The State of West Bengal & Ors.) was filed in the Hon'ble High Court, Calcutta. Upon hearing the Learned Advocates of both parties (Mr. Phalguni Sarkar, Advocate for the petitioners and Mr. Manik Das, Advocate for the respondents), Hon'ble Justice Ruma Pal was pleased to dispose of the said application by directing the Deputy Commissioner of Police, Lalbazar, Calcutta to treat the above mentioned writ application as a representation and to dispose of the same within a period of six weeks from the date of service of a copy of the instant order with a copy of the writ petition after giving the representative of the petitioners an opportunity of being heard and with a reasoned order[31].

In the writ petition No.3262 of 1998, pursuant to the High Court's order of consideration of all aspects by the appropriate administrative authority, the Deputy Commissioner of Police (Traffic), Calcutta, upon hearing the parties rejected the prayer of the writ petitioners, viz. the rickshawpullers, on 4th May, 1998. This rejection was made in view of the desire of the then Chief Minister of West Bengal and in view of the National Human Right's Commission's observation to abolish the hand pulled rickshaw as pulling of a rickshaw by a man was an inhuman matter and also as because the number of licensed rickshawpullers i.e. 1800 had come down to 1750 because of non renewal of licence by them and due to serious traffic problem in Calcutta and for replacing hand pulled rickshaws by auto rickshaws[32].

The All Bengal Rickshaw Union and others, being aggrieved and dissatisfied by the order passed by the Deputy Commissioner of Police (Traffic), Lalbazar, preferred another writ application under Article 226 of the Constitution of India before the High Court, Calcutta which was numbered as *W.P. No.9758 of 1998*. In this writ application the petitioners prayed for directions upon the respondents to quash and or recall the impugned order dated 04.05.1998, to issue fresh licence and or renew the pullers' licence in accordance with the provisions of Calcutta Hackney Carriage Act and restraining the respondents from taking any penal action against the rickshawpullers for not having valid licence till disposal of the instant application[33].

The writ application No.9758 of 1998 (All Bengal Rickshaw Union & Ors. State of West Bengal & Ors.) was heard by Hon'ble Justice Amitava Lala and he delivered his judgement on 14.12.1999. According to the contention of the petitioners about 6000 licenced rickshaws were plying in Calcutta in 1998-99 having prior licence issued by the Hackney Carriage department before 1950 and since then no single licence was issued to any person pursuant to their respective applications. 24,000 rickshawpullers obtained puller's licence from the licencing authority as per the provisions of the Calcutta Hackney Carriage Act, 1919. But the Hon'ble Court observed that the strength of fresh or renewed licenced rickshaw pullers had come down to 1700 from 24000 due to the adamant attitude of the Registering Authority in not renewing the old licences. Since 1950 no new licence was issued by the concerned authority and no fresh or renewed licence was issued since 1990. Hon'ble Justice Lala further observed that the impugned order dated 4$^{th}$ May, 1998 was passed as a government policy in view of the desire of the Hon'ble Chief Minister of West Bengal but the administrative authority did not consider properly the grievance of the petitioners. With these observations Hon'ble Court set aside the Annexure "F" viz. the order dated 04.05.1998 passed by the Deputy Commissioner (Traffic) Lalbazar. The Court further directed that the rickshaws which were running under appropriate licence would not be seized till the completion of the direction given by this Court. The State Authority was directed to form an appropriate high powered committee in this respect for the purpose of fruitful result on the basis of the judgement and guidelines given under the order of this Court. The Committee will be formed within a period of two weeks from date, will call upon the associations for the purpose of prima facie discussion and for the purpose of formation of a cell and thereafter a cell will be formed within a period of two weeks to conclude the course of action within a period of another eight weeks from the date of formation of the cell on the following guidelines:-

(a) All Bengal Rickshaw Union, petitioner No.1 herein will be directed by the cell to furnish names and particulars of the rickshawpullers or the owners of such rickshaws under a prescribed format to be supplied by the cell when the association will make an identification and verification about the authenticity and place such names with particulars under the format with their recommendations for the purpose of consideration by the cell.

(b) Consideration will be made by the cell basically on the following lines :

(i) A proposal will be made to such rickshaw pullers or owners as to whether they are inclined to go back to their home-state, if they come from other state or states, and in such circumstances, the cell will certify them about tenure of work, financial condition priority etc. for the purpose of their rehabilitation there and negotiate with their counterpart of such state or states so that the same may be sympathetically considered by the authorities or the state or states for their appropriate rehabilitation therein on the basis of such certificate giving priority over others.

(ii) A fresh proposal will be made to all of them for the purpose of rehabilitation and financial assistance in the nature of loan or certification of loan by other agencies with recommendation for the purpose of purchasing an auto rickshaw or for doing business similar in nature.

(iii) By allowing the movement of rickshaw pullers in the restricted manner for the sake of tourism in the market area or in the area nationally declared as heritage or tourist zone of Calcutta and fixing the appropriate rate for the livelihood to keep the symbol of 'City of Joy' alive. The instant writ petition was disposed of[34].

Being aggrieved by and dissatisfied with the *judgement and order dated 14.12.1999 in W.P. No.9758 of 1998* passed by Hon'ble Justice Amitava Lala, the appellants, viz. the State of West Bengal & Ors. preferred an appeal before the Hon'ble Court against the All Bengal Rickshaw Union & Ors. numbered as *F.M.A. No. 175 of 2003*[35].

*On 13.06.2013 this appeal* numbered as *F.M.A. No.175 of 2003* was dismissed for want of prosecution by the divisional bench of Hon'ble Chief Justice Arun Misra and Hon'ble Justice Joymalya Bagchi as none appeared before the Hon'ble Court on behalf of the appellants viz. the State of West Bengal & Ors[35a].

The All Bengal Rickshaw Union & Ors. being aggrieved by the inaction of the Kolkata Municipal Corporation and its authorities in renewing the certificate of enlistment for the handpulled rickshaws as per the provisions of section 199 of the Kolkata Municipal Corporation Act since the Calcutta Hackney Carriage Amendment Act, 2006 was passed, preferred a writ application being *W.P. No.1035 (W) of 2007* (All Bengal Rickshaw Union & Ors. Vs. The State of West Bengal & Ors.) before the Hon'ble High Court, Calcutta. Hon'ble Justice Dipankar Datta after hearing the Learned Counsels of both parties on 27.09.2007, 04.10.2007 and 09.10.2007 delivered his judgement and order on 16.10.2007 wherein the Hon'ble Judge held that the action of the corporation in not considering and disposing of the applications for renewal of certificates of enlistment received by it from the members of the petitioner No.1, viz. the All Bengal Rickshaw Union either by granting or refusing it, to be unjustified, wrongful and harassing act. The decision on the applications filed has not been given on extraneous grounds. The Corporation is directed to proceed to consider only those application received by it in accordance with law and in the light of the observations contained above and to pass appropriate orders on all the applications as early as possible but positively within six weeks from the date of receipt of a copy of this judgement and order. the writ petition succeeds to the extent indicated above[36].

The Kolkata Municipal Corporation being aggrieved by and dissatisfied with the judgement and order passed by Hon'ble High Court on 16.10.2007, in connection with W.P. No.1035 of 2007, preferred an appeal being *A.P.O.T. No.60 of 2008* (Kolkata Municipal Corporation & Ors. Vs. All Bengal Rickshaw Union & Ors.). The said appeal was heard by Hon'ble Justice Kalyan Jyoti Sengupta and Hon'ble Justice Abdul Ghani on *24.06.2009.* The Hon'ble Judges after hearing, were pleased to pass an order as follows:- "The Corporation, in terms of the direction of the Learned Trial Judge, shall proceed to consider only those applications received by it in accordance with law. The appeal and the application accordingly stand disposed of[37]".

In compliance with the judgement and order passed by the Hon'ble High Court on 24.06.2009, *the Chief Manager (Licence), Kolkata Municipal Corporation*, heard the matter of All Bengal Rickshaw Union representing the owners and pullers of jin-rickshaws on 10.10.2009 and 29.10.2009 in his chamber in Kolkata Municipal Corporation. The All Bengal Rickshaw Union & Ors. duly attended the hearing and filed a written submission before the Chief Manager (Licence) on 10.10.2009. After hearing the Learned Advocate appearing for the All Bengal Rickshaw Union, the Chief Manager (Licence) rejected the prayer of the petitioners by observing that though in the proviso to section 199(2) of Kolkata Municipal Corporation Act, 1980, clear reference has been made for production of necessary licence/permission as may be required under the Kolkata Municipal Corporation Act, 1980, before the Municipal Commissioner for obtaining an Certificate of enlistment, as and when the writ petitioner would be able to produce permission/clearance from the Police Authorities for plying Jin-Rickshaws within the City of Kolkata, Licence Department, KMC would move to Municipal Commissioner for giving necessary approval for granting of certificates of enlistment for the Jin-Rickshaws as per proviso of Section 199(2) of the KMC Act, 1980. Without production of such permission/clearance from the Police Authorities Licence Department of KMC would not be in a position to grant/issue Certificate of Enlistment for the profession "owner of Jin-Rickshaws" in terms of Section 199(1) read with Schedule IV of KMC Act, 1980. The Chief Manager (Licence) further opined that the Kolkata Municipal

Corporation does not issue any trade licence. As per provision of Section 199 (1) of KMC Act, 1980, KMC only issues Certificate of Enlistment upon receipt of application to facilitate running of any trade/profession/calling as applied for. Hence the profession of the owner of Jin-Rickshaws' as mentioned in Schedule IV read with Section 199(1) of KMC Act, 1980 can only be deemed to be authorized, if necessary permission/clearance from police authorities can be produced before Kolkata Municipal Corporation[38].

Being aggrieved by and dissatisfied with the impugned order dated 29.10.2009 passed by the Chief Manager (Licence) of Kolkata Municipal Corporation, the All Bengal Rickshaw Union and others preferred another writ application (All Bengal Rickshaw Union & Ors. Vs. The State of West Bengal & Ors.) numbered as *W.P. No.239 of 2010* before the Hon'ble High Court, Calcutta and prayed for cancellation of the order dated 29.10.2009, cancellation of any notification/ restriction/or imposition issued by the Police Authority with regard to plying of jin-rickshaw within the city of Kolkata and for directions upon the respondents to forthwith issue certificate of Enlistment in terms of section 199 of the Kolkata Municipal Corporation Act, 1980 in favour of petitioner no.1[39].

In connection with the writ application, W.P. No. 239 of 2010 *Dilip Bandyopadhyay, Deputy Commissioner of Police (Traffic), Kolkata* sworn an affidavit on 23rd March, 2010 wherein he specifically denied all the contents of the instant writ application and stated that a reply to the letter dated 12.01.2010 sent by the All Bengal Rickshaw Union to the police authority, had been communicated to the General Secretary, All Bengal Rickshaw Union vide memo No.01/Law/T.P. dated 06.02.2010. In this letter the Deputy Commissioner of Police (Traffic), Kolkata intimated Mukhtar Ali, General Secretary of All Bengal Rickshaw Union, having office at 51, Chittaranjan Avenue, Kolkata – 700012, that, "in terms of notification No. TP/738/G dated 18th April, 1994, plying of cycle rickshaw in the streets or public places in Kolkata is prohibited. Of late an amendment in Hackney Carriage Act, 1919, by omitting the term rickshaw from the principal act, has been enacted and given effect of such amendment into act from 01.07.2007 vide Notification No.3251-P dated 28.06.2007[40]".

The writ application W.P. No.239 of 2010 was heard by the Hon'ble High Court and *Hon'ble Justice Debangsu Basak* in his judgement and order passed on *22nd April, 2015* was pleased to set aside the impugned order dated 29.10.2009 passed by the Chief Manager (Licence) of Kolkata Municipal Corporation. The Hon'ble Court observed that "earlier notifications issued by the Police Authorities restricting the movement of rickshaws within the city of Kolkata, does not prevent plying of Jin-Rickshaws in the city of Kolkata in its entirety but it regulates and restricts plying at different locale at different point of time. The Hon'ble Court further directed the Chief Manager (Licence) to consider and decide the grant of application made by the writ petitioners or any persons entitled thereto for grant of certificate of enlistment for plying Jin-Rickshaw in the city of Kolkata in terms of the Judgement and order dated June 24, 2009 and the observations made herein. The Chief Manager (Licence) was further directed by the Hon'ble Court to give a reasonable opportunity of hearing to the writ petitioners and also hear such other person which he deems necessary. The Chief

Manager (Licence) will pass a reasoned order thereto and will communicate this order to the writ petitioners. The Chief Manager (Licence) will endeavour to dispose of the proceedings within a period of six weeks from the date of making of the fresh application for certificate of enlistment. The writ petitioners are granted opportunity to apply afresh before the Municipal Authorities with such application. The Chief Manager (Licence) will consider such applications in terms of the directions herein. With the aforesaid directions W.P. No.239 of 2010 is disposed of[41]."

The Licence officer (H.Q.), Kolkata Municipal Corporation, holding office at 5, S.N. Banerjee Road, in compliance with the order of Hon'ble Justice Debangsu Basak, sent a notice to the secretary, ABRU (All Bengal Rickshaw Union) to appear before the *Chief Manager (Licence)* on 20.06.2015 at 12.00 noon at conference Room No.2 of CMO Buildings at 5, S.N. Banerjee Road, Kolkata – 700013. This hearing notice was dated 03.06.2015. On *29.06.2015* Mr. Mukhtar Ali, General Secretary and Sri Kashinath Pal, treasurer of All Bengal Rickshaw Union attended the hearing while the officials from Traffic Department, Kolkata Police, Lalbazar and Officer-in-Charge, Hackney Carriage Branch along with the officials of Law Cell, Traffic Department, Kolkata Police also attended this hearing. Officials of Licence Department present in the hearing contended that without further amendment of Hackney Carriage (Amendment) Act, 2006 and further insertion of the term 'Jin-Rickshaw' in the Principal Act, there is no scope for Licence Department, to issue/renew licences for 'Jin-Rickshaw' commonly known as handpulled rickshaw. Thus the prayer of the handrickshaw pullers for issuance and renewal of licence was rejected by the Chief Manager (Licence)[41a].

From the above discussion of the provisions of the Calcutta Hackney Carriage Act, 1919 implemented by the British Government in 1919 for regulating the trade of hackney carriages including handpulled rickshaws, the subsequent amendment of this Act in 2006 by the Left Front Government of the State of West Bengal, the ban imposed on the handrickshaw and the Chief Manager's (Licence, Kolkata Municipal Corporation) refusal to issue or renew the licence of the hand rickshaw pullers on the plea that the term 'Jin Rickshaw' is not mentioned in the Calcutta Hackney Carriage (Amendment) Act, 2006, it is crystal clear that the main issue regarding the issuance and renewal of licence to the handrickshaw pullers and owners has been left unsolved. Nor the series of litigations filed before the High Court, Calcutta from the year 1998 till 2010 by the All Bengal Rickshaw Union against the State of West Bengal could render a final solution to the issue of renewal and/or grant of fresh licence to the handrickshaw pullers since the year 2006. As a consequence a large number of unlicensed handpulled rickshaws are plying on the streets, lanes and by-lanes of Calcutta at present while the ban on the handrickshaws has not yet been put into action by the State Government. Thus the legal stand or status of the hand rickshaw pullers is uncertain, unstable and indefinite. It is the sole responsibility of the State Government to take necessary steps, as required for solving this issue of the rickshaw pullers fully and finally on a permanent basis, which would give relief to the hand rickshaw pullers and handrickshaw owners.

***Notes and References***

1. The Calcutta Hackney Carriage Act, 1919, Bengal Act 1, 1919, p. 303.
2. The Calcutta Hackney Carriage Act, 1919, Bengal Act I of 1919, proviso added by W.B. Act 36 of 1948, p. 321.
3. The Calcutta Hackney-Carriage Act, 1919, op.cit.
4. The Calcutta Hackney Carriage Act, Bengal Act, 1 of 1919, p. 323.
5. The Calcutta Hackney Carriage Act, 1919 (Bengal Act 1 of 1919) p. 325.
6. Abstracts of Proceedings of the Government of Bengal for the month of June, 1919, Political Department, File No. P. 10–H-3(1), No.1674, P.J. dated Calcutta, 13th May, 1919, p.25, State Archives, Kolkata.
7. Abstracts of Proceedings of the Government of Bengal, Political Department, File No. 77 PJ-D, dated Darjeeling, 27th May, 1919, p. 25, State Archives, Kolkata.
8. Abstracts of Proceedings of the Government of Bengal, Political Department, File No. P. 10-H-3(5) No. 4275-G-46-13 dated 31st May, 1919, pp. 26-27, State Archives, Kolkata.
9. Proceedings of the Government of Bengal, Police Department, June, 1931, File P. 10 H-2 Proceedings 336 & 337, State Archives, Kolkata.

9a. Proceeding of the Government of Bengal, Police department May 1932, File P 10 H-1, proceedings 177 & 178, File P 10-H-2 B May, 1931, Nos. 336 & 337, State Archives, Kolkata.

10. Proceedings of the Government of Bengal, Police Department, September, 1933, Notification dated Calcutta, 21st August, 1919, State Archives, Kolkata.
11. Notification dated 21st August, 1919, op.cit., State Archives, Kolkata.
12. Proceedings of the Government of Bengal, Police Department, March, 1932, Calcutta Police Notification, dated 6.1.1932, pp. 43-44, 45, 51, 53, 54, 61-63, 64-67, 69, 71, State Archives, Kolkata.

13. Proceedings of the Government of Bengal, Police Department, File No.462/69 H.C.B. dated Calcutta, 25th July, 1932, State Archives, Kolkata.
14. Proceedings of the Government of Bengal, Police Department, File No. P.10-H-2(2) of 1932, No. 4786 P.1 dt. 30th September, 1932 Calcutta, State Archives, Kolkata.
15. Proceedings of the Government of Bengal, Police Department, File No. P.10-H-2(3) of 1932, No. 478./ H.C.B. dated Calcutta, 26th October, 1932, States Archives, Kolkata.
16. Proceedings of the Government of Bengal, Police Department, Notification No.1084 M. dt. 31st March, 1920, and Notification No. 5949 P1, dt. 30th November, 1932, State Archives, Kolkata.
17. Proceedings of the Government of Bengal, Police Department, File No. PH-10-2 (11) of 1932, No.953 P1 dt. Calcutta, 2nd March, 1933, State Archives, Kolkata.
18. Proceedings of the Government of Bengal, Police Department August, 1935, File No. P-10 H-3 of 1934, Notification by G.P. Hogg, Chief Secretary to the Government of Bengal, State Archives, Kolkata.
19. Proceedings of the Government of Bengal, Police Department June, 1936, File No. P 10-H-2, B. Proceedings 162 & 163, June, 1936, State Archives, Kolkata.
20. Proceedings of Government of Bengal, Police dept., July 1936, File P. 10H-2 of 1935, Proceedings 87 to 92, July, 1936, B, State Archives, Kolkata.
21. Proceedings of Government of Bengal, Police Dept., 1929-30 file No. P. 10 H/30, (1-6), State Archives, Kolkata.
22. Proceedings of Government of Bengal, Police Dept., 1930-31 File No. PH10/31, 1-2, State Archives, Kolkata.
22a. The Calcutta Gazette, Government of West Bengal, Home Department, Transport, dated 24.12.1965.

23. ***The Statesman*** Newspaper, Calcutta, dated 17.08.2005.

24. ***The Statesman*** Newspaper, Calcutta, dated 17.08.2005.

25. ***The Statesman***, Calcutta, dated 20.07.2006.

26. ***The Statesman***, Calcutta, dated 20.07.2006.

27. ***The Statesman***, Calcutta, dated 05.12.2006.

27a. ***The Statesman***, Calcutta, dated 30.01.2006.

28. The Kolkata Gazette, Extraordinary, published on 13th February, 2007, Part-III – Acts of West Bengal, Legislature.

29. Police Regulations, Calcutta, 1968, Vol-I, Chapter-V, Kolkata, 2018.

29a. Personal Interview of Mr. Subroto Bandyopadhyay, O.C., Hackney Carriage Department, taken by the author on 16.03.2023 in his office at Munshi Prem Chand Sarani, Kolkata– 700021.

30. Letter dated 18.09.1987 written by Gopal Chandra Ghosh, Advocate, High Court, Calcutta to the Commissioner and Deputy Commissioner of Police (Traffic) Lalbazar Calcutta-1, copy of which is Annexure "C" to the W.P. No.9758 of 1998 (Certified Copy).

31. Lawyer's letter dated 20.03.1998 written by Phalguni Sarkar, Advocate, High Court, Calcutta to the Deputy Commissioner of Police, specially appointed by the State Government for the purpose of carrying out the provisinos of the Calcutta Hackney Carriage Act, 1919.

32. Copy of the observation of D.C.T.P. dated 04.05.1998 in compliance with the order passed by Hon'ble Justice Ruma Pal in W.P. No. 3262 of 1998 marked as Annexure "F" in W.P. 9758 of 1998. (Certified Copy).

33. Certified copy of the writ application No.9758 of 1998.

34. Certified copy of the judgement and order passed by Hon'ble Justice Amitava Lala on 14.12.1999.

35. Certified copy of the Memorandum of Appeal from the

Original order numbered as M.A.T. No.1239 of 2000 (The State of West Bengal & Ors. Vs. All Bengal Rickshaw Union & Ors.)

35a. Certified copy of the judgement and order passed by Hon'ble Chief Justice Arun Mishra & Hon'ble Justice Joymalya Bagchi on 13.06.2013 in F.M.A. No.175 of 2003 (State of W. Bengal –Vs- All Bengal Rickshaw Union & Ors.).

36. Certified copy of the judgement and order in W.P. No. 1035 of 2007 (All Bengal Rickshaw Union & Ors. Vs. State of West Bengal & Ors.) passed by Hon'ble High Court on 16.10.2007.

37. Certified copy of the judgment and order dated 24.06.2009 passed by Hon'ble Justice Kalyan Jyoti Sengupta and Md. Abdul Ghani in G.A. No.1565 of 2009 with A.P.O. No.108 of 2008, W.P. No.1035 of 2007.

38. Certified copy of the order dated 29.10.2009 passed by the Chief Manager (Licence) of Kolkata Municipal Corporation, Annexure 'P-4' annexed to the writ petition i.e. 239 of 2010 (All Bengal Rickshaw Union & Ors. Vs. The State of West Bengal & Ors.)

39. Certified copy of writ application W.P. No.239 of 2010 (All Bengal Rickshaw Union & Ors. Vs. The State of West Bengal & Ors.)

40. Certified copy of W.P. No.239 of 2010 (All Bengal Rickshaw Union & Ors. Vs. The State of West Bengal & Ors.), affidavit of Dilip Bandopadhyay annexed to the writ petition.

41. Certified copy of the Judgement and order dated 22.04.2015 passed by Hon'ble Justice Debangsu Basak in W.P. No.239 of 2010 (All Bengal Rickshaw Union & Ors. Vs. The State of West Bengal & Ors.)

41a. Copy of the order passed on 29.06.2015 by the Chief Manager (Licence), Kolkata Municipal Corporation in the matter of issuance and renewal of licence to the handrickshaw pullers & owners.

# Chapter VI

## Conclusion

Handpulled rickshaws are a permanent feature of Calcutta's traditional aura. These quaint little vehicles have been plying through the streets, lanes and bye-lanes of Calcutta for more than 100 years. They were first introduced in 1888 in Shimla by the Chinese immigrants, who arrived in Calcutta in the 19th and the first half of the 20th centuries. The handpulled rickshaws are undeniably an integral and vital part of the city's culture and an icon of this metropolis. These rickshaws have also acquired a special status in terms of antiquity which can never be substituted by anything else.

These rickshaws have a whole bounty of advantages to offer, nothing in the least detrimental to the populace. They are the only means of transport in waterlogged streets and they navigate through the serpentine lanes of Calcutta where a four wheeler or three wheeler vehicle cannot enter[1].

Calcutta and the handpulled rickshaw are synonymous to a large extent as it evokes memories of compassion, nostalgia, loss and deprivation. The rickshaw never faded into oblivion but surprisingly it continues to fascinate the foreign traveller who visits this City of Joy and never forgets to take a picture of a handpulled rickshaw along with its puller.

Handrickshaws are important providers of both transport and employment in the city of Calcutta. In Calcutta the street pattern and size are dense and often narrow not suited to large motorised transport modes and sometimes even inaccessible other than by a handpulled rickshaw. The handpulled rickshaw is pollution free and is useful for commuting educational and social travel as well as for carrying goods. There rickshaws provide employment and financial support to hundreds of migrant workers who fill the jobs of rickshaw pullers. The rickshaws also provide cheap, reliable and consumer friendly transport options. They are particularly useful for women, the elderly, the frail and disabled and the rickshaw-wallahs are always ready to serve the customers at any hour of the day or night, and will carry passengers during the worst of monsoons through the waterlogged streets and lanes. But above all the rickshaw-wallahs will take children to and from school with personal care and reliability[2].

The hand rickshaws entered passenger service in Calcutta in 1914, though jin-rickshaw, a Japanese term meaning 'manually powered vehicle' was first invented by a missionary in Japan in 1871. Subsequently in 1914 the Chinese migrants in Calcutta obtained the permission of the British Government to operate hand rickshaws for passenger transport. In the 20$^{th}$ century which is supposedly the era of mechanised transport, the hand rickshaw has disappeared in other cities but in Calcutta the man-powered rickshaw continues to hold its own against the competition of trains, buses, trams, taxis, mini-buses, auto-rickshaws[3] and metro railway.

The primary role of the handpulled rickshaw is to offer comfortable, reliable and effectively fast conveyance over short distance, with provision for the carriage of luggage and for the care of vulnerable passengers. In medium and low density urban areas the hand rickshaws play a marginal role while in north and central Calcutta, these rickshaws are a normal adjunct to social and commercial life. The handrickshaw though primarily a passenger cart, it is also used for transporting accompanied and unaccompanied goods. Its capacity for goods is not great either in terms of weight or volume and there is no facility for securing goods to the chaise. Typical loads are vegetables, boxes of shoes, paper for printers, ironmongery, small furniture and traveller's baggage. Near all the central markets in Calcutta such as Sealdah, Machuabazar and Posta one can see large number of hand rickshaws carrying goods to and fro. In Howrah there are a number of old handrickshaws whose hoods have been removed for solely using them for the purpose of carrying industrial goods[4].

Though rickshaw pulling is a socially acceptable activity, in Calcutta society, however a rickshaw puller has a very low status. Around 10% pullers have their families living with them in Calcutta at present as their monthly income is low and many of them are found living in slums in the north, central and south Calcutta while the rest of them stay overnight on the footpath. Rickshaw pulling seems to be the first choice of the unskilled and illiterate rural migrants from Bihar whereas migrants from the districts of Bengal will first try their luck in hawking or other kind of work and treat rickshaw pulling as the last resort[5].

No one can deny the problems inherent in the

rickshaw trade – the work is hard and low paid, the pullers are poorly organised, there is no structural fare system and licencing is abused. Yet the hand rickshaws provide a valuable service to the city. But many things need to be tackled – rickshaw technology, licencing, operating conditions, traffic management welfare issues and a structured fare system[5a].

Compared to the low income of the handrickshaw puller, the owner of a modest fleet of rickshaws, even when employing an agent (sardar) to supervise its day to day operation, makes a much better living than his pullers do. Many owners also have other side business in order to increase their income and they do not depend solely on the rickshaw trade for their sustenance[5b].

**The issue of Rehabilitation of the handrickshaw pullers and owners**

The hand pulled rickshaws are undeniably an itegral and important part of Calcutta culture. They are pollution free, cheap transport compared to other mode of transport such as taxis, three wheelers and so on and they remain the only means of transport in waterlogged streets and serpentine and narrow lanes of Calcutta. Yet the State Government of West Bengal represented by the then Chief Minister Buddhadeb Bhattacharjee banned the handpulled rickshaw by an amendment of the Calcutta Hackney Carriage Act, 1919, which came into force in the year 2007.

Mr. Bhattacharjee took this decision on humanitarian grounds. "It is inhuman for a man to carry another man. Moreover handpulled rickshaws are still an unfortunate symbol of the city to many foreigners as are its beggars and shanties. This has to change." But Mr. Buddhadeb Bhattacharjee and his Transport Minister, Mr. Subhas Chakraborty contradicted each other over the question of rehabilitating handrickshaw pullers. Mr. Bhattacharjee said, "we are planning to adopt the Chinese model of cycle rickshaws as an alternative to handpulled rickshaws. The rickshaw pullers will be trained accordingly. On the other hand Mr. Chakraborty ruled out allowing cycle-rickshaws to ply on city streets as they would disrupt traffic. "Traffic in Kolkata will come to a standstill if cycle rickshaws start plying within city limits", he said. Instead, the Transport Minister hinted that the State would assist such rickshaw pullers to obtain bank loans to run LPG driven auto-rickshaws. But licences for these would be issued after thorough verification, he said[6].

We come to know from **the Statesman** dated 17.08.2005 that the All Bengal Rickshaw Union demanded a rehabilitation package from the State Government. Mr. Mukhtar Ali, the then Vice-President of the Union, said, "Not only the pullers, the government will have to rehabilitate all the people associated with the profession like the owners and supervisors of the rickshaws." The Union leaders claimed that currently 18,000 rickshaws ply on the city roads and 6000 owners and 800 supervisors have a secondary income from the rickshaws. Most of the pullers hail from Muzaffarpur, Gaya, Darbhanga, Baishali district in Bihar, Hazaribag, Giridih districts in Jharkhand, North 24 Parganas and South 24 Parganas districts in West Bengal. They live either in clusters under inhuman conditions or lie on the footpaths of the city roads. Hand rickshaws are the best and the cheapest mode of transport in the waterlogged roads and during emergency, even at night, they are at the doorstep to carry patients to the hospital[7].

However those engaged in the manufacture and repair of rickshaws seem to be the worst hit. They will have no source of income, once the proposed amendment of the Calcutta Hackney Carriage Act, 1919 is put into effect. Md. Nizamuddin, who has been repairing and manufacturing rickshaws for the last 20 years in a small workshop besides the B.B. Ganguly Street, said, "We heard of rehabilitation packages been declared for the pullers, but what will happen to us? Our expertise is limited to the repairing and manufacturing of these rickshaws only ......". Majority of the rickshaw pullers like Hiralal, Suraj Prasad, Rajender wanted to shift from the 'inhuman' mode to some better options like cycle rickshaws. Mr. Bikash Ranjan Bhattacharya the then Mayor, also welcomed the move. He said "the rickshaw pullers will be provided with rickshaws designed by the authorities of IIT, Kharagpur which will ply within the alleys and by-lanes in the usual routes in the city[8]".

But curiously enough on 2nd August, 2006 Mr. Bikash Ranjan Bhattacharya contradicted his previous statement and declared that KMC will neither renew the licences of handpulled rickshaws nor rehabilitate the rickshaw pullers. He categorically stated that rehabilitation was the "responsibility of the State Government". There are about 17,000 rickshaw pullers in the city and taking into account their families nearly 70,000 people are dependent on the trade. The licences of the hand pulled rickshaws that expired on 2nd August will not be renewed, thus rendering them illegal. Mr. Bhattacharya said, "The rickshaws will have to go as their use is inhuman. There is no use raising this issue as they will not be brought back[9]".

Thus the fate of the handrickshaws was sealed

by the erstwhile Left Front regime that banned "colonial relics" on 15th August 2005, after terming them as inhuman and degrading[9a]. Though the Calcutta Hackney Carriage Amendment Bill, 2006, had been legally challenged, the government refused to renew the licences of hand pulled rickshaws.

The Left Front Government utterly failed to provide any rehabilitation package to the rickshaw pullers while the Kolkata Municipal Corporation stopped the renewal or issuance of licences to the handrickshaw pullers across the city since 2006. As a consequence an estimated 18,000 hand pulled rickshaws were rendered illegal. Mayor, Mr. Bikash Ranjan Bhattacharya said, "Alternative proposals like engaging these rickshaw pullers as parking attendants, setting up self help groups or imparting vocational training were mooted but the options were shot down by the Unions[10]".

Although the State Government in 2006 tried permanently banning handpulled rickshaws in the city of Calcutta by the passing of Calcutta Hackney Carriage (Amendment) Bill, but it was never implemented. Nothing has changed after the change of government in 2011, in respect of hand rickshaws, though blank promises were made by the government for replacing the licenced hand pulled rickshaws with e-rickshaws.

Mr. Mukhtar Ali, General Secretary of the All Bengal Rickshaw Union informed us that after the State Government changed hands in 2011, he, on behalf of the Union and the hand rickshaw pullers sent an application to the present Chief Minister, Sm. Mamata Banerjee wherein he prayed for rehabilitation of hand rickshaw pullers. In 2014 the Chief Minister called him and Mr. Ali along with other rickshaw owners met her in her office at Nabanna, 14th floor, 325, Sarat Chatterjee Road, Shibpur, Howrah – 711102 and they showed her a design of e-rickshaw. Thereafter Mr. Alapan Bandyopadhyay, the then Chief Secretary called Mr. Ali in his office at Tranport Bhawan where two/ three meetings were held and a draft resolution was made on Gatidhara Type-2-a·package for rehabilitation. But thereafter there was no response from the Chief Minister's office. A scheme for rehabilitation of owners and pullers of handrickshaws (Alternative Livelihood-cum-Rehabilitation Scheme) was sent by Mr. Ali. Sm. Mamata Banerjee way back on 15th December, 2014, announced a scheme of Green Rickshaw (E-Rickshaw) but it was never implemented. In December, 2015, the Transport Department of the Government of West Bengal, having its office at 12, R.N. Mukherjee Road, Kolkata – 700001 drafted a resolution wherein the guidelines of the Scheme styled as Gatidhara – Type-II (Alternative livelihood-cum-Rehabilitation Scheme for owners/pullers of hand rickshaws, were framed. This scheme provided for operating environmental friendly 3-seater (2 passengers and one driver) mechanically driven e-rickshaws and operable with rudimentary driving skills in selected areas or on predefined routes in Kolkata. The transport department of West Bengal government shall be the administrative department for this project. Financial assistance will be provided by the State Government. But this resolution was never published in the official Gazette. On 27th June, 2016, Mr. Ali along with members of ABRU (All Bengal Rickshaw Union) met the then Transport Minister and presented him a complete Dossier containing the draft of the scheme or resolution prepared by the transport department. A 'detailed Data' of about 6000 registered owners of hand pulled rickshaws was submitted in this department. On 15.12.2016, Mr. Ali again submitted the scheme for rehabilitation of owners/pullers of handrickshaws in the office of Sm. Mamata Banerjee, the Hon'ble Chief Minister of West Bengal[11].

Mr. Mukhtar Ali further stated to the author that E-Rickshaw Bill had been passed. But it was not formally and finally implemented by the State Government. Since then a lot of correspondences, meetings and personal discussions took place with various authorities connected with the subject matter of hand rickshaws vide letters dated 14.12.2018, 25.09.2020 and 28.06.2021 but till date there has been no progress in this matter of rehabilitation. On 28.09.2021 Mr. Mukhtar Ali sent a Memento/Souvenir depicting a model of an age old handrickshaw as a symbol of heritage to Sm. Mamata Banerjee on behalf of ABRU (All Bengal Rickshaw Union)[12].

It is reported in the **Telegraph** newspaper dated 16.12.2014 that Mamata Banerjee announced that her government would replace around 6000 hand pulled rickshaws with battery-driven e-rickshaws, thus removing a British-era symbol that some call slavery. "The association of handpulled rickshaws came to my residence on Saturday. Today (Monday) they met me here ....... We have accepted their proposal. The association will find out every detail about the green rickshaws, who manufactures them, at what price they will supply and other such things", the Chief Minister said at Nabanna. "Once they let us know we will buy the green rickshaws for them. We are willing to do this as rehabilitation for the 6000 owners and the 6000 rickshaw pullers.

Twelve thousand families will benefit directly from this", she added. Parliament on Monday cleared an amendment to the Motor Vehicles Act, 1988 to include provisions for e-rickshaws. This will pave the way to lift the ongoing loan on e-rickshaws in the Capital and allow the Bengal Government to frame its own rules, based on the central law[13].

According to the amendment an e-rickshaw "is a special battery operated vehicle having three wheels and intended to provide last mile connectivity". The rule specifies that the vehicle should not carry more then four passengers. The net power of its motor should not be more than 2000 watt and the maximum speed of the vehicle should not exceed 25 Kmph[14].

Subsequently on 09.02.2024 Mukhtar Ali on behalf of ABRU sent another representation to the Chief Minister praying for rehabilitation of handpulled rickshawpullers and owners. Thereafter on 21.02.2024 Mukhtar Ali along with 5/6 rickshaw owners met the Transport Minister in his office in the transport building at Mango Lane. The Minister's secretary directed Mr. Ali to give a fresh data about the number of present handrickshaw pullers in Calcutta as well as the model of the e-rickshaw which the hand rickshawpullers want for rehabilitation. Mukhtar Ali confirmed that the e-three wheeler cycle rickshaws will be battery operated with the capacity to travel 10 to 12 kilometers only in the lanes and by-lanes of the city. He also informed the author that he has contacted an agency at Dhulaghat for the purpose of constructing the model of the aforesaid e-cycle rickshaw. Mukhtar Ali has also requested the State Government for grant of a health card and free ration for the handrickshaw pullers. Furthermore Mr. Ali has started a welfare fund for the handrickshaw pullers for the purpose of spending the money, collected through donation, for the health, ration of the pullers and for the education of the children of the pullers. However the application dated 21.02.2024 praying for rehabilitation of handrickshaw pullers and owners is still pending for disposal before the transport Secretary[15].

**Should hand rickshaws be banned ?**

The removal of hand rickshaws from Calcutta will have an immediate catastrophic effect on the well being of hundreds of thousands of people already struggling on the economic margin. The livelihood of the pullers would be destroyed with little scope of finding any alternative employment since the handrickshaw pullers are unskilled and cannot do any technical work. Their dependants in rural Bihar, Bengal and Jharkhand would likewise suffer. Those men who are employed in the manufacture and maintenance of rickshaws would also lose their livelihood. The hand rickshaw is currently under valued and under-utilised as a means of transport. Redefining the rickshaw so that it can play a more secure role in Calcutta's transport system involves tackling the rickshaw technology, licensing and operating conditions, traffic management and welfare issues. The importance of rickshaws requires that the threats against them should be removed and that their role in the overall transport system of Calcutta should be maximised. Indeed sustainable development and sustainable transport require that hand rickshaws be given a secure position in Calcutta's transport system and a new role in an integrated transport plan[16].

The handrickshaw trade is large scale and well adopted to the peculiar transport problems and travel needs of Calcutta. Banning these rickshaws would impoverish the pullers and owners, inconvenience their patrons and have bad side effects such as increasing road accidents for children and inhibiting business. Handrickshaws are safe amongst pedestrians, they are more maneuverable, they park more compactly and they accelerate and decelerate more briskly[17].

The handpulled rickshaw which has been plying on the streets, lanes and by-lanes of Calcutta for over 100 years, has become an important and remarkable cultural heritage of the City of Joy. The rickshawallas have been rendering good service to the society of Calcutta, being pollution free, cheap mode of transport and reliable transport for carrying school children to and from their home and school, being the only mode of transport in the monsoon season when the city's lanes and roads are waterlogged and also reliable for carrying patients, old and sick as well as reliable for carrying goods. "As a rickshawpuller is unskilled and unabel to do any technical work it is a human right for him to pull a rickshaw for his sustenance", opined Mukhtar Ali, the General Secretary of the All Bengal Rickshaw Union.

In many countries of the world such as in China, Japan, Hong Kong, Vietnam (Ho-Chi-Min City), Singapore and Cambodia hand rickshaws are still in use. Though less in number, these hand rickshaws are specially popular among the tourists. Still now tourists in the city of Kurasiki in Japan enjoy a rickshaw ride for the purpose of sightseeing and photography[18].

It is hightime that the State Government should take necessary steps for the rehabilitation of hand rickshaw pullers and owners in Calcutta by putting into effect the amendment to the Motor Vehicles Act, 1988 which includes provisions for e-rickshaws, and by introducing sufficient number of battery operated three wheeler e-rickshaws which the pullers will operate only in the lanes and by-lanes of the city. E-rickshaws will thus provide an alternative means of livelihood to the handrickshawpullers and thereby save them from verging towards abject poverty. The rickshaw owners will, in turn, get an alternative source of income from buying such e-rickshaws and renting them to the pullers.

It is also the sole responsibility of the State Government to save the hand pulled rickshaw by taking necessary steps for promoting the handrickshaw as a tourist attraction for local sightseeing like visiting the heritage buildings and other historical sights in Calcutta located within short distance. Handpulled rickshaws, a significant heritage of Calcutta should not be allowed to pass into the pages of history but these rickshaws should be permitted by the State Government to be preserved for the posterity as these rickshaws have been playing a vital role in the transport system of Calcutta for more than a century and thereby they have become an important and integral part of the socio-cultural and transport history of Calcutta.

***Notes and References***

1. **The *Statesman*** (newspaper), dated 1.2.2007, Kolkata.
2. Whiteleg, John, & Williams Nick, 'Save the Riksha', an article posted on Poverty Environment Net on 21.11.2006.
3. Thomas T.H., a report "Rickshaws in Calcutta" in Unnayan, AIIPH, February, 1981, Calcutta, p.1.
4. Thomas, T.H., 'Rickshaws in Calcutta', op. cit., pp. 7, 12, 13
5. Thomas, T.H., 'Rickshaws in Calcutta', op. cit., p. 22

5a. **The *Statesman*** newspaper, '8th Day', 10th December, 2006, Calcutta.

5b. Field study of the handrickshaw owners made by the author in 2022 and 2023.

6. **The *Statesman*** newspaper, dated 17.08.2005, Calcutta.

7. **The *Statesman***, dated 17.08.2005.

8. **The *Statesman***, op. cit., dated 17.08.2005.

9. **The *Statesman*** dated 3.8.2006, Calcutta.

9a. **The *Statesman***, dated 07.07.2011, Calcutta.

10. **The *Statesman***, dated 30.1.1995, Calcutta

11. Personal Interview of Mukhtar Ali taken by the author on 29.11.2022 in his office at 56, Beck Bagan Row, Kolkata – 700017.

12. Personal Interview of Mukhtar Ali, op.cit.

13. ***The Telegraph*** (newspaper) dated 16.12.2014, Calcutta.

14. ***The Telegraph***, dated 16.12.2014, Calcutta.

15. Personal Interview of Mukhtar Ali taken by the author on 30.03.2024 in the ABRU's office at 51, Chittaranjan Avenue, Kolkata – 700012.

16. Whiteleg, John & Williams, Nick, 'Save the Ricksha', an article on *Poverty Environment Net*, 21.11.2006.

17. Thomas T.H. Dr., 'Rickshaws in Calcutta', a report by Dr. Thomas and Workers of Unnayan, February, 1981, Calcutta. pp. 49-51.

18. ***Sambad Pratidin***, Bengali newspaper, dated 22nd August, 2005, p. 6.

## BIBLIOGRAPHY

**I. Primary Sources** : **Unpublished**

**A Archival Sources** : Materials in West Bengal State Archives, Calcutta


1. Abstracts of proceedings of the Government of Bengal for the month of June, 1919, Political Department (Police), File P-10 H-3, Proceedings No.21 to 26, dated 06.06.1919.
2. Proceedings of the Government of Bengal, Proceedings No.21, File No. P10-H-3(1) No.1674 P.J. dated Calcutta, 13th May, 1919.
3. Proceedings of the Government of Bengal, File No.1675 P.J. dated Calcutta, 13th May, 1919.
4. Proceedings of the Government of Bengal, Proceedings No.23, File No.77 P.J. – D, dated Darjeeling, 27th May, 1919.
5. Proceedings of the Government of Bengal, Proceedings No.24 File No.1907 P.J. dated Calcutta, 31st May, 1919, p. 26.
6. Proceedings of the Government of Bengal, Political Department Proceedings No.25, File No. P10-H-3(5), No.4275-G 46-13 dated Calcutta, 31st May, 1919. pp. 26-27.
7. Abstracts of Proceedings of the Government of Bengal File No. P10-H-4 of 1929, Proceedings 32 to 34, Order dated 22nd March, 1930,

Police Department.

8. Proceedings of the Government of Bengal, File No.P10-H-4(1) of 1929, No BK-411 dated Calcutta, 23rd December, 1929, Police Department.
9. Proceedings of the Government of Bengal, File No.10370, dated Calcutta, 30th November, 1929.
10. Proceedings of the Government of Bengal, Police Department, File No.P10-H-2, Proceedings Nos.336 & 337, June, 1931.
11. Proceedings of the Government of Bengal, Police Department, March, 1932, Calcutta Police Notification, pp. 43-44, 45, 51, 53, 54, 61, 63-64, 65-67, 68-69, 71.
12. Proceedings of the Government of Bengal, Police Department, File P10-H-Z of 1930, B, August, 1931 (Nos.142 to 147) (permanent), December 1931.
13. Proceedings of the Government of Bengal, Police Department, File No.P10-H-3, Proceedings 241 to 242, December, 1931.
14. Proceedings of the Government of Bengal, Police Department, File No. P10-H-1, Proceedings Nos.177 & 178, May, 1932.
15. Proceedings of the Government of Bengal, Police Department, File No. P10-H-2 B, May, 1931, Proceedings Nos.336 & 337.
16. Government of Bengal, Police Department, File No. P10-H/30, 1-6, 1930, letter No. $\frac{9150}{46-13}$ from the office of the Commissioner of Police, Calcutta to the Chief Secretary to the Government of Bengal, Calcutta.
17. Proceedings of the Government of Bengal, Police Department, 1931, File No. $\frac{\text{P10M/30}}{2}$ dated 28.03.1931.

18. Government Proceedings of Bengal, Police Department File No. PH10/31 (1-2).
3

19. Government Proceedings of Bengal, Police Department, File No. TG/940 dated 1st September, 1931.

20. Government Proceedings of Bengal, Police Department, File No. $\frac{P10-H/31}{3}$ 1931, letter No. $\frac{7580}{46-13}$ dated 21st September, 1931.

21. Proceedings of Government of Bengal, Police Department, File No. P10-H-2(1) of 1932 dated Rangoon, 1st August, 1932.

22. Proceedings of the Government of Bengal, Police Department, September, 1933. File No. P10-H-Z(1) of 1932 dated Rangoon, 1st August, 1932 Notification, dated Calcutta, 21st August 1919, by the Deputy Commissioner of Police, Hackney Carriage Department.

23. Proceedings of Government of Bengal, Police Department, File No.69 H.C.B. dated 19th July, 1932, Calcutta. File No. L/J dated 25th July, 1932, Calcutta.

24. Proceedings of Government of Bengal, Police Department, File No.462/69 H.C.B. dated 25th July, 1932, Calcutta.

25. Proceedings of Government of Bengal, Police Department, File No. P10-H-Z(2) of 1932, No.4786 P1, dated 30th September, 1932, Calcutta.

26. Proceedings of Government of Bengal, Police Department, File No. P10-H-Z(3) of 1932, No.478/H.C.B. dated 26th October, 1932, Calcutta.

Notification No.1084M dated 31st March, 1920 (amendment to Hackney Carriage By-laws).

27. Proceedings of Government of Bengal, Police Department, File No. P10-H-Z(4) of 1932, No. AL/J dated Calcutta, 17th November, 1932.
28. Proceedings of Government of Bengal, Police Department, File No. P10-H-Z(11) of 1932, No. 953 P1 dated Calcutta, 2nd March, 1933.
29. Proceedings of Government of Bengal, Police Department, File No. P10-H-4 of 1934, Proceedings 231 to 235 (permanent), Abstract of Matters of Routine of the Government of Bengal for the month of March, 1935, Police Department.
30. Proceedings of the Government of Bengal, Police Department, August, 1935, File No. P10-H-3(2) of 1934.
31. Proceedings of Government of Bengal, Police Department, June, 1936, File No. P10-H-Z, B Proceedings 162 & 163, June, 1936.
32. Proceedings of Government of Bengal, Police Department, July, 1936, File No. P10-H-Z of 1935, B Proceedings 87 to 92, July, 1936.
33. Proceedings of Government of Bengal, Police Department, November, 1936, File No. P10-H-1, B Proceedings 385 to 387, November, 1936.

**B. Unpublished Archival Records in Kolkata Police Museum and Archives :**

1. KPM(SB) 00851/05, File No. S.W. 822/1939, Government of Bengal, Police Department, Confidential - on the Calcutta Rickshaw Association.
2. KPM/SB/01036/05, File No. SW-994 of 1944 Memo No. M.V. 11662, H.C.B. File No. G100(1), Calcutta Richshaw Mazdoor Union, the Bengal

Rickshaw Mazdoor Union & Bengal Rickshaw Union.

3. File No. S.W. 994 of 1944, Letter NO.6151-L.C. dated 14th December, 1945, letter from the Addl. Labour Commissioner, Bengal to the Secretary, Calcutta Rickshaw Mazdoor Union.

**C. Other unpublished Archival Records :**

1. Report and Audited Accounts of All Bengal Rickshaw Union for the year 1999.
2. Report and Audited Accounts of All Bengal Rickshaw Union for the year 2000.
3. Certified copy of the Writ Petition No. 9758 of 1998 and a letter dated 18.09.1987 written by Gopal Chandra Ghosh, Advocate, High Court, Calcutta to the Commissioner and Deputy Commissioner of Police (Traffic) Lalbazar, Calcutta – 700001, a copy of which is Annexure 'C' to this writ petition.
4. Lawyer's letter dated 20.03.1998, written by Phalguni Sarkar, Advocate, High Court, Calcutta to the Deputy Commissioner of Police.
5. Copy of the observation of D.C.T.P. dated 04.05.1998 marked as Annexure 'F' in Writ Petition No.9758 of 1998 (All Bengal Rickshaw Union & Ors. –Vs- State of West Bengal & Ors.).
6. Certified copy of the judgment & order passed by Hon'ble Justice Amitava Lala on 14.12.1999 in Writ Petition No.9758 of 1998 (All Bengal Rickshaw Union & Ors. –Vs- State of West Bengal & Ors.).
7. Certified copy of the Memorandum of Appeal numbered as M.A.T. No.1239 of 2000 (The State of West Bengal & Ors. –Vs- All Bengal Rickshaw Union & Ors.).

8. Certified copy of the judgment & order passed by Hon'ble Chief Justice Arun Mishra & Hon'ble Justice Joymalya Bagchi on 13.06.2013 in F.M.A. No.175 of 2003 (State of West Bengal & Ors. Vs- All Bengal Rickshaw Union & Ors.).
9. Certified copy of the judgment & order in Writ Petition No.1035 of 2007 (All Bengal Rickshaw Union & Ors. –Vs- State of West Bengal & Ors.) passed by Hon'ble Justice Dipankar Dutta on 16.10.2007.
10. Certified copy of the judgment & order dated 24.06.2009 passed by Hon'ble Justice Kalyan Jyoti Sengupta and Md. Abdul Ghani in G.A. No.1565 of 2009 with A.P.O. No.108 of 2008 & W.P. No.1035 of 2007.
11. Certified copy of the order dated 29.10.2009 passed by the Chief Manager (Licence) of Kolkata Municipal Corporation, Annexure 'P-4' annexed to the writ petition No.239 of 2010 (All Bengal Rickshaw Union & Ors. –Vs- The State of West Bengal & Ors.).
12. Certified copy of the Writ Petition No.239 of 2010 (All Bengal Rickshaw Union & Ors. –Vs- The State of West Bengal & Ors.).
13. Affidavit of Dilip Bandopadhyay annexed to the Writ Petition NO.239 of 2010.
14. Certified copy of the judgment & order dated 22.04.2015 passed by Hon'ble Justice Debangsu Basak in W.P. No.239 of 2010.
15. Certified copy of the order passed on 29.06.2015 by the Chief Manager (Licence), Kolkata Municipal Corporation.

**II. Interviews and Field Survey :**

1. Interview with Bablu Haldar, a handrickshaw

puller at the rickshaw stand outside the Gariahat Market on 30.10.2022.

2. Interview with Sunil Sardar, a handrickshaw puller at the rickshaw stand outside the Gariahat Market on 30.10.2022.
3. Interview with Sona Mondal, a handrickshaw puller at the rickshaw stand outside the Gariahat Market on 30.10.2022.
4. Interview with Jamiruddin Jamal, a handrickshaw puller at the rickshaw stand outside the New Market (Hogg Market) at Lindsay Street on 13.11.2022.
5. Interview with Sk. Nazim, a handrickshaw puller at the rickshaw stand outside the New Market (Hogg Market) at Lindsay Street on 13.11.2022.
6. Interview with Moh. Tohid, a handrickshaw puller at the rickshaw stand outside the New Market (Hogg Market) at Lindsay Street on 13.11.2022.
7. Interview with Nandu Shaw, a handrickshaw puller at the rickshaw stand at 10, Cornfield Road on 13.11.2022.
8. Interview with Misri Lal Yadav, a handrickshaw puller at the rickshaw stand at 10, Cornfield Road on 13.11.2022.
9. Interview with Sudhan Das, a handrickshaw puller at the rickshaw stand at 10, Cornfield Road on 13.11.2022.
10. Interview with Budar Das, a handrickshaw puller at the rickshaw stand at 10, Cornfield Road on 13.11.2022.
11. Interview with Haricharan Yadav, a handrickshaw puller at the rickshaw stand near

Shyambazar-Bagbazar crossing in north Calcutta on 20.11.2022.

12. Interview with Prakash Shaw, an owner of handpulled rickshaws at 7, Nebubagan Lane, Calcutta – 700003 on 20.11.2022.

13. Interview with Mahesh Yadav, a hand rickshaw puller at the rickshaw stand near Shyambazar-Bagbazar crossing in north Calcutta on 22.11.2022.

14. Interview with Sudeswar Yadav, a handrickshaw puller at the rickshaw stand near Shyambazar-Bagbazar crossing in north Calcutta on 22.11.2022.

15. Interview with Anwar Hussain, a handpulled rickshaw owner cum Sardar in his rickshaw khatal at 28/1, Beniapukur Road on 11.12.2022.

16. Interview with Kishan Deb Yadav, a handrickshaw puller cum owner and Sardar at 219/1A, Picnic Garden Road, Calcutta – 700039 on 12.12.2022 & on 02.04.2024.

17. Interview with Parameswar Sharma, a handpulled rickshaw craftsman in the rickshaw repairing garage at 219/A1, Picnic Garden Road, Calcutta – 700039 on 12.12.2022.

20. Interview with Tenny Sharma, a craftsman of handpulled rickshaw in the rickshaw repairing garage at 219/A1, Picnic Garden Road, Calcutta – 700039 on 12.12.2022.

21. Interview with Dhurup Lal Shaw, an owner of handpulled rickshaws in his house at 40, P.G.S. Basu Road, Calcutta – 700039 on 12.12.2022.

22. Interview with Ramdhani Sharma, a handpulled rickshaw owner cum Sardar in his rickshaw

khatal (garage) at 236, B.B. Ganguly Street, Bowbazar on 13.12.2022 & on 23.12.2022.

23. Interview with Moh. Israil, a handrickshaw puller in the rickshaw garage at 236, B.B. Ganguly Street on 13.12.2022.

24. Interview with Moh. Saleem, a handrickshaw puller in the rickshaw garage at 236, B.B. Ganguly Street on 13.12.2022.

25. Interview with Ram Ekbal Sharma, a handrickshaw craftsman in the rickshaw garage at 236, B.B. Ganguly Street on 13.12.2022.

26. Interview with Chandreswar Sharma, a handrickshaw craftsman in the rickshaw garage at 236, B.B. Ganguly Street on 13.12.2022.

27. Interview with Mukhtar Ali, General Secretary of All Bengal Rickshaw Union (ABRU) and an owner of handpulled rickshaw, in his office at 56, Beck Bagan Row, Calcutta – 700017 on 29.11.2022 and in the office of ABRU at 51, Chittaranjan Avenue, Calcutta – 700012 on 30.03.2024.

28. Interview with Swarna Singh, Executive Secretary of ABRU and an owner of handpulled rickshaw, in the office of ABRU at 51, Chittaranjan Avenue, on 10.12.2022.

29. Interview with Moh. Mukhtar, a handrickshaw puller in the rickshaw garage at 28/1, Beniapukur Road on 11.12.2022.

30. Interview with Sukkan Ram, a handrickshaw puller in the rickshaw garage at 28/1, Beniapukur Road on 11.12.2022.

31. Interview with Mr. Gautam Gupta (OSD), Deputy Commissioner, Police, Traffic department, in

his office at Lal Bazar, Kolkata Police Headquarters, on 01.06.2022.

32. Interview with Mr. Subroto Bandyopadhyay, Officer-in-Charge, Hackney Carriage department of Kolkata Police in his office at Munshi Prem Chand Sarani, Calcutta - 700021 on 16.03.2023.

33. Interview with Sri Kashinath Paul, an owner of handpulled rickshaw and the Vice-President of All Bengal Rickshaw Union in the rickshaw garage at 236, B.B. Ganguly Street on 23.12.2022.

34. Interview with Swapan Kumar Roy, an owner of handpulled rickshaw in the rickshaw garage at 226, B.B. Ganguly Street on 23.12.2022 & on 27.12.2022 in his rickshaw garage at 21/2A, Mahendra Goswami Lane, Kolkata - 700006.

35. Interview with Tulsi Shaw, a handrickshaw puller at the rickshaw stand at Bethun Row & Ramdulal Street crossing on 27.12.2022.

36. Interview with Sanjay Yadav, a handrickshaw puller at the rickshaw stand at Bethun Row & Ramdulal Street crossing on 27.12.2022.

37. Interview with Rajkumar Ghosh, a handrickshaw owner near his residence at 28A, Nanda Mullick Lane, Kolkata - 700006 on 27.12.2022.

38. Interview with Munilal Mahato (nee Rajjak) a handrickshaw puller cum sardar on 27.12.2022 at 130, Ramdeo Sarkar Street, Kolkata - 700006.

39. Interview with Debu Yadav, a handrickshaw puller on 29.12.2022 at 130, Ramdeo Sarkar Street, Kolkata - 700006.

40. Interview with Mohammad Yunus, a handrickshaw puller cum owner cum sardar in his residence at 27, Aga Mehendi Street on 23.01.2023.
41. Interview with Joykumar Rana, a handpulled rickshaw owner in his residence at 15, Sankrapara Lane, Bowbazar, Kolkata – 700012 on 24.01.2023.
42. Interview with Santosh Shaw, a handrickshaw owner and also the owner of "Shaw Jewellery" Shop at 90, B.B. Ganguly Street, on 28.01.2023.
43. Interview with Indrajit Sharma, a craftsman of handpulled rickshaws in the rickshaw garage at 15, Sankrapara Lane, Kolkata – 700012 on 28.01.2023.
44. Interview with Umesh Sharma, a craftsman of handpulled rickshaws in the rickshaw garage at 15, Sankrapara Lane, Kolkata – 700012 on 28.01.2023.
45. Interview with Nagen Haldar, a craftsman of handpulled rickshaw in his residence at 1B, Jadu Mitra Lane, Kolkata – 700004 on 04.02.2023.
46. Interview with Rajkumar Thakur, a handpulled rickshaw owner in his residence at 1B, Jadu Mitra Lane on 04.02.2023.
47. Interview with Sukul Sharma, handpulled rickshaw owner cum rickshaw craftsman at 22A, Rajendra Mullick Street, Kolkata – 700007 on 11.02.2023.
48. Interview with Dr. Mohammad Iqbal, a handpulled rickshaw owner at the rickshaw stand at 26A, Balaram Bose Ghat Road, Kolkata – 700025 on 23.07.2023 & on 25.07.2023 at 2/C, Tiljala Road, in his chamber.

49. Interview with Debnath Kamat, a handrickshaw puller at the rickshaw stand at 26A, Balaram Bose Ghat Road, Kolkata – 700025 on 23.07.2023.

50. Interview with Jaleswar Sharma, a handrickshaw craftsman in the rickshaw garage of Dr. Moh. Iqbal at 2/C, Tiljala Road on 25.07.2023.

51. Personal visit and survey of the handpulled rickshaw garage of Prakash Shaw at 7, Nebubagan Lane, Caclutta – 700003 on 20.11.2022.

52. Personal visit and survey of the handrickshaw garage of Anwar Hussain at 28/1, Beniapukur Road on 11.11.2022.

53. Personal visit and survey of the handrickshaw khatal of Kishan Deb Yadav at 219/1A, Picnic Garden Road, Calcutta – 700039 on 12.12.2022.

54. Personal visit and survey of the handrickshaw garage of Ramdhani Sharma at 236, B.B. Ganguly Street, Bowbazar on 13.12.2022.

55. Personal visit and survey of handrickshaw garage of Joykumar Rana and Santosh Shaw at 15, Sankrapara Lane, Bowbazar, Calcutta – 700012 on 24.01.2023.

56. Personal visit and survey of handrickshaw garage of Dr. Mohammad Iqbal at 2/C, Tiljala Road on 25.07.2023.

**III. Secondary Sources :**

**Books & Articles :**

1. Ghosal, Soumya Sarkar, an article on handpulled rickshaws in Calcutta published in website www.sahapedia.org dated 9th December, 2019.

2. The Calcutta Samaritans & Action Aid, Kolkata, 'A Report on Hand Rickshaw Pullers of Kolkata', Calcutta, 2003.
3. Siddique, M.K.A.(ed), 'Aspects of Society and Culture in Calcutta', Calcutta, 1982.
4. Thomas, Dr. T.H. & Unnayan AIIPH, A report, 'Rickshaws in Calcutta', Calcutta, 1981.
5. Whiteleg, John & Williams, Nick, An article 'Save the Riksha', posted on Poverty Environment Net, 21.11.2006.
6. Rules & Bye-laws of All Bengal Rickshaw Union, Calcutta, 1934.
7. Wheeler, Tony & Richard, I'Anson, 'Chasing Rickshaws', Australia, 1998.
8. The Calcutta Hackney Carriage Act, 1919, Bengal Act, 1 of 1919.
9. West Bengal Act, XXXV of 2006, The Calcutta Hackney Carriage (Amendment) Act, 2006, Calcutta, 2007.
10. Rahman, Z.(ed), Police Regulations, Calcutta, 1968, Vol. 1, Kolkata, 2018.


**IV. Journals and Newspapers :**

**Journals :**


1. Calcutta Police Gazette, April 21, 1994, Part-II, Order of the Governor dated 17th December, 1965.
2. The Kolkata Gazette, February 13, 2007, Part-III, West Bengal Act XXXV of 2006.
3. The Kolkata Gazette, June 28, 2007, amendment of the Calcutta Hackney Carriage Act, 1919.
4. The Modern Review, Vol. XLIX, 'Bhadralok Rickshawpullers', Calcutta, May 1931.

5. Mainstream, March 27, 1982, Calcutta.

6. Mainstream, May 8, 1982, Calcutta.

**Newspapers :**

1. The Statesman, dated 17.08.2005, Calcutta.
2. The Statesman, 'Notebook', dated 22.08.2005, Calcutta.
3. The Statesman, 'Ricky in the City', the issue : 'Handpulled rickshaws are an affront to human dignity', dated 29.08.2005, Calcutta.
4. The Statesman, 8th Day, 'The Long Run', December 10, 2006, Calcutta.
5. The Statesman, 'Requiem for hand-pulled rickshaw', 5th December, 2006, Calcutta.
6. The Statesman, 'Rickshaws out for good, not hawkers', 3rd August, 2006, Calcutta.
7. The Statesman, 'Hand-pulled rickshaws may get a burial today', 20th July, 2006, Calcutta.
8. The Statesman, 'Their Last Days', 1st February, 2007, Calcutta.
9. The Statesman, 'Rickshaws on their way out', 7th August, 2007.
10. The Statesman, 'Rickshaw Ruckus', 18th May, 2008, Calcutta.
11. The Statesman, dated 30th January, 2009, Calcutta.
12. The Statesman, 'Rickshaw is part of city's heritage', 26th June, 2011, Calcutta.
13. The Statesman, 'Rickshawpullers to seek Didi's help', 25th June, 2011, Calcutta.
14. The Statesman, 'KMC to provide subsidy for solar powered rickshaws', 11th October, 2011, Calcutta.
15. The Statesman, 'Rickshawpullers to get back

livelihood', 7th July, 2011, Calcutta.

16. Sambad Pratidin (Bengali Newspaper) dated 22nd August, 2005, Calcutta.
17. Bartaman (Bengali Newspaper) dated 22nd December, 2011, Calcutta.
18. Bartaman (Bengali Newspaper) dated 20th April, 2012, Calcutta.
19. Telegraph 'After rickshaw blot, e-rickshaw bane', 16th December, 2014, Calcutta.
20. Bartaman (Bengali Newspaper), dated 16th December, 2014, Calcutta.
21. Provat (Hindi Newspaper) dated 27th March, 2013, Calcutta.
22. Sanmarg (Hindi Newspaper) dated 16th December, 2014, Calcutta.
23. Provat, dated 13th February, 2015, Calcutta.

# Index

**C**

**D**

**S**

Kashinath Paul, President of All Bengal Rickshaw Union

Mukhtar Ali, the General Secretary of All Bengal Rickshaw Union

Swarna Singh, Executive Secretary of All Bengal Rickshaw Union sitting inside the office of the Union

The rickshaw owners & pullers in a rally near Mahatma Gandhi's statue

Dr. Mohammad Iqbal, a hand rickshaw owner standing at the rickshaw stand at Balaram Bose Ghat Road, Kol - 29

Dr. M. Iqbal sitting in his chamber at 2/C Tiljala Road

Jaleswar Sharma, a rickshaw craftsman sitting inside the rickshaw garage at 2/C Tiljala Road

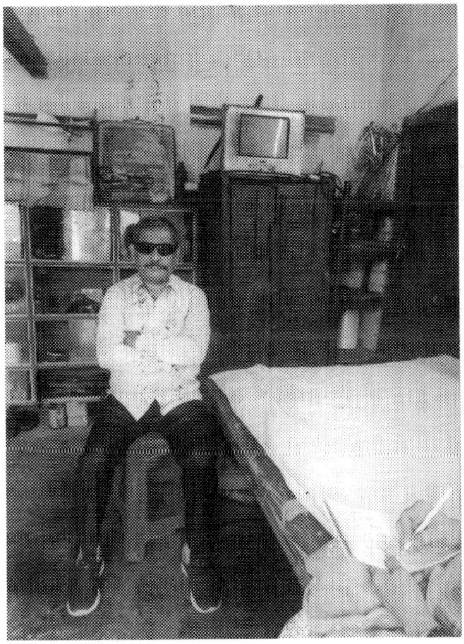

Anwar Hossain, a rickshaw owner sitting in his room in the rickshaw khatal at 28/1 Beniapukur Road

A rickshaw pullers lying on a cot inside the khatal at 28/1 Beniapukur Road

Inside view of the rickshaw khatal
at 28/1 Beniapukur Road

A dormitory inside the khatal
at 28/1 Beniapukur Road where
the rickshaw pullers stay

Moh. Mukhtar, a rickshaw puller inside
the khatal at 28/1 Beniapukur Road

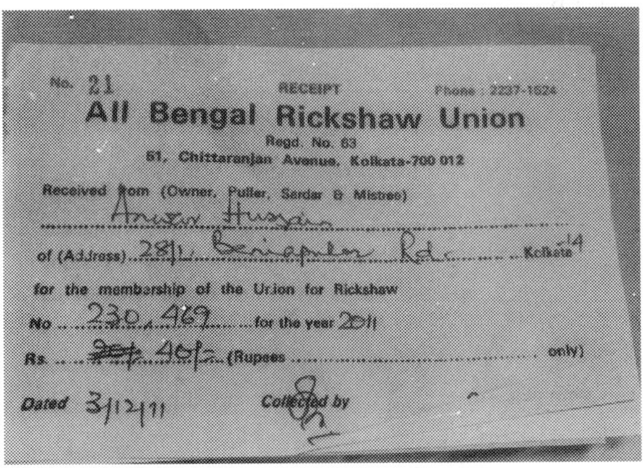

No. 21 RECEIPT Phone : 2237-1524

**All Bengal Rickshaw Union**

Regd. No. 63

51, Chittaranjan Avenue, Kolkata-700 012

Received from (Owner, Puller, Sardar & Mistree)

of (Address) 28/1, Beniapukur Rd. Kolkata-14

for the membership of the Union for Rickshaw

No 230, 469 for the year 2011

Rs. ~~30/-~~ 40/- (Rupees ..................... only)

Dated 3/12/11 Collected by

Receipt of membership fee of
All Bengal Rickshaw Union

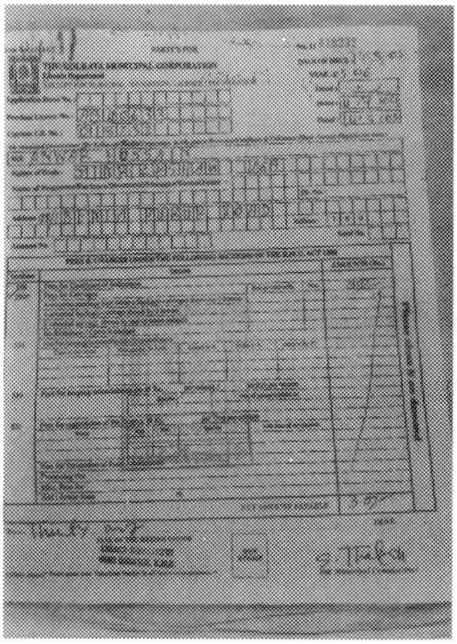

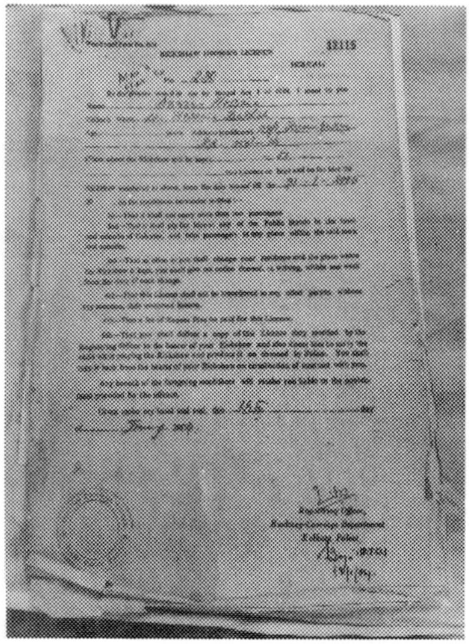

A copy of Corporation Licence of Anwar Hossain

Prakash Shaw, a handrickshaw owner & author interviewing the rickshawpullers at the rickshaw stand at Shyambazar crossing

Outside view of the rickshaw khatal at 7, Nebubagan Lane, Kol - 3

Inside view of the rickshaw khatal at 7, Nebubagan Lane, Kol - 3

Dhurup Shaw & Kishan Deo Yadav, rickshaw owners sitting in the compound of the house of Dhurup Shaw at 40P, Dr. G. S. Bose Road, Kol - 39

Outside view of rickshaw garage of Kishan Deo Yadav at 219/1A, Picnic Garden Road

Inside view of rickshaw garage
of Kishan Deo Yadav with rickwhaw
craftsman Tenny Sharma

Tenny Sharma working
in the garage at 219/1A, Picnic
Garden Road

Rickshaw craftsman working
in the rickshaw garage of Dhurup Shaw
at 40P, Dr. G. S. Bose Road, Kol - 39

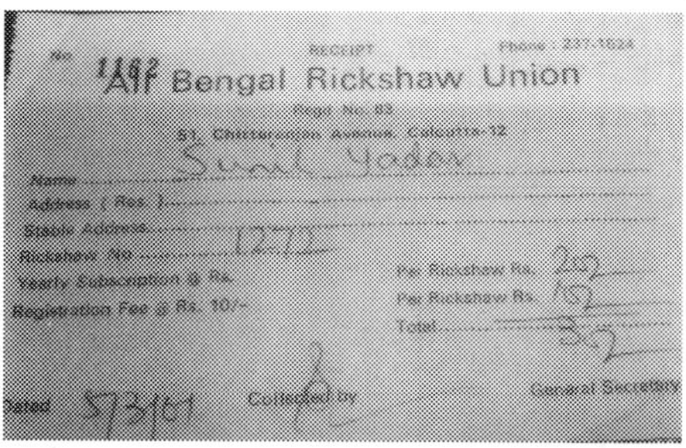

RECEIPT

All Bengal Rickshaw Union

Name Sunil Yadav
Address ( Res. )
Stable Address
Rickshaw No 1272
Yearly Subscription @ Rs. Per Rickshaw Rs. 20
Registration Fee @ Rs. 10/- Per Rickshaw Rs. 15
Total 35

Dated 5/3/01 Collected by General Secretary

Yearly subscription of
a member of ABRU

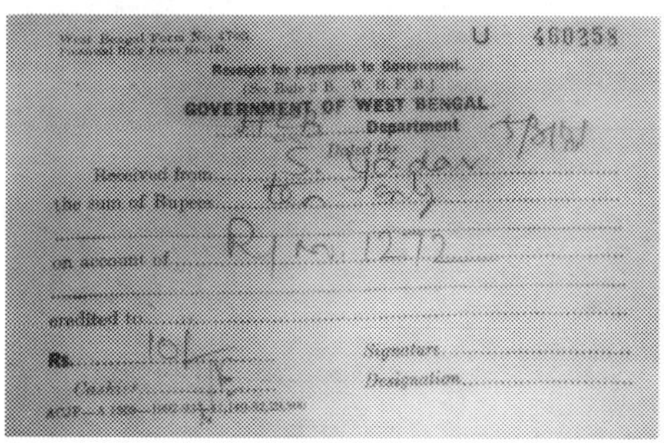

GOVERNMENT OF WEST BENGAL

Department

Received from S. Yadav
the sum of Rupees
on account of R/no. 1272
credited to
Rs. 10/- Signature
Cashier Designation

Handrickshaw puller's
fee paid in the Hackney
Carriage department

Moh. Yunus, a hand rickshaw owner, at 27, Aga Mehandi Street

Inside view of a room where rickshaw pullers stay at 27, Aga Mehandi Street

Rickshaws of Moh. Yunus parked on the street near his residence

Rickshawpullers waiting for passengers outside the New Market at Lindsay Street

A rickshawpuller waiting for passengers outside the New Market at Lindsay Street

Rickshawpuller Debnath Kamat & another at the rickshaw stand near Mitra Institution at Bhawanipur

Rickshawpuller Babu Haldar at the rickshaw stand near Gariahat Market

Rickshawpuller Sunil Sardar at the rickshaw stand near Gariahat Market

Joy Kumar Rana, a handrickshaw owner

Santosh Shaw,
a handrickshaw owner

Inside view of rickshaw khatal
at 15, Sankrapara Lane, Bowbazar

Rickshaw craftsman, Indrajit Sharma & Umesh Sharma in the rickshaw garage at 15, Sankrapara Lane, Bowbazar

Registration number of a handpulled rickshaw

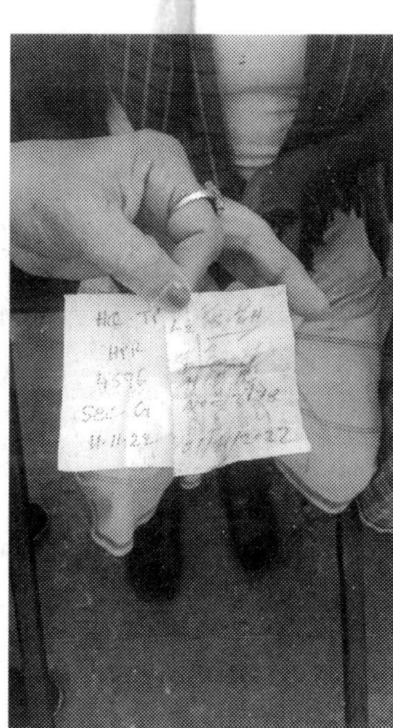

Handwritten slips given by the local traffic police to the rickshaw puller showing the petty case number

Swapan Kumar Roay & Rajkumar Ghosh, rickshaw owners

Ramdhani Sharma,
a rickshaw owner